THE
FOUR
ROOMS

THE FOUR ROOMS

AN IN*QUEER*Y ON SEXUAL FREEDOM AND WELL-BEING

DAVID WICHMAN

ONBrand Books
an imprint of W. Brand Publishing
NASHVILLE, TENNESSEE

The Four Rooms: An InQueery on Sexual Freedom and Well-being by David Wichman – First Edition

j.brand@wbrandpub.com

W. Brand Publishing

www.wbrandpub.com

Cover and interior design: JuLee Brand | designchik

Available in Paperback, Kindle, and eBook formats.

PB: 979-8-89503-012-7

eBook: 979-8-89503-013-4

Library of Congress Control Number: 2025901709

Non-Fiction / Men's Health / LGBTQIA

CONTENTS

.

THE GUEST HOUSE

This being human is a guest house.
Every morning a new arrival.

A joy, a depression, a meanness,
some momentary awareness comes
as an unexpected visitor.

Welcome and entertain them all!
Even if they're a crowd of sorrows,
who violently sweep your house
empty of its furniture.
Still, treat each guest honorably.
He may be clearing you out
for some new delight.

The dark thought, the shame, the malice,
meet them at the door laughing,
and invite them in.

Be grateful for whoever comes,
because each has been sent
as a guide from beyond.
—Rumi

A word about words: I'm a work in progress and ask for leniency when it comes to the world of language. I'm also writing this book for an incredibly diverse audience—one with a wide range of experiences, attitudes, histories, and sensitivities to the various sexual topics addressed here.

I know language matters, but even then, I'll no doubt struggle to write with perfect inclusivity. Language is dynamic—it changes over time, sometimes faster than the speed of publishing. A word or phrase that's considered inoffensive today might be interpreted differently by the time this book comes out.

So, I encourage you to read this book in a way that serves you best. Swap out any language you find troublesome for words that feel better suited to you.

You'll notice I use the term "queer," as it encapsulates so many versions of our NB-LGBTQIA+2 experience. We took back this word long ago, stripping it of the power those who weaponized it once held over us. I reclaim it with my whole chest.

"Queer people don't grow up as ourselves, we grow up playing a version of ourselves that sacrifices authenticity to minimize humiliation and prejudice. The massive task of our adult lives is to unpick which parts of ourselves are truly us and which parts we've created to protect us."
—Alexander Leon

If there's one thing I'm passionate about, it's the subject of sexual freedom and well-being. My passion to help as many people as possible discover more sexual freedom in their lives is what fuels my message.

In my work, I've consistently seen men struggle with their sexuality, their self-worth, and their search for intimacy. As a gay male escort for more than seventeen years, I've had the privilege of working with men from all walks of life.

Many of the men who've hired me over the years were sexually skilled and fully at ease with their sexuality and well-being; they simply wanted to hire me as part of their sexual self-care. Then there were those who felt broken, unacceptable, and a sense of not belonging to their core. They often reached out to me steeped in fear, reluctance, sometimes even as a last resort.

One thing I've noticed among a great many of these men, regardless of their life circumstances, is the impact of the shame they carry from a religious upbringing, a disapproving family, and a society that constantly sends the message that there's something wrong with queer men simply because of their sexuality. Some of us may be more immune to that kind of messaging than others, but most of us live with it.

I've also seen men cracked wide open. I've witnessed raw ecstasy, deep sadness, sexual catharsis, and sexual stuckness. I've seen the game we all play with reality—playing roles and wearing masks. Yet nothing feels as vulnerable as being naked in a room with only our desires, a longing for touch, and the lifetime of walls we've built to protect ourselves.

What I've noticed is that when breakthroughs happen, they don't come from eliminating some paralyzing core belief, like you might read in a book or see in a movie. Instead, they emerge from acknowledging those struggles—and even more, embracing them as a natural part of being a sexual person.

Witnessing such bravery and vulnerability is a privilege. Nearly two decades as a sex worker have shown me that my role wasn't just about fulfilling men's sexual desires. It was about creating a space where feelings of not-enoughness or the illusion of inadequacy could exist alongside a satisfying, erotic, and sometimes emotional experience. I am here to make space for the men I worked with to come as they are—not just for sexual breakthroughs but also for the fearful, aloof fumbling and the awkwardness that sex can bring—masks, insecurities, and all.

Some of these men I've known for many years, and we've cultivated relationships that run deep and profound, some lasting until the end of their lives. Others, I've seen only once and never again. What I've seen and learned from them—alongside my own inner observations—forms the foundation of what

I'm sharing here. These are the men I hope this book will speak to the most.

I have no doubt that those with vibrant sex lives and a wealth of experience might read this book and not resonate with its content—and that's perfectly OK. Still, I invite you to look for what is useful to you and leave the rest. I am also acutely aware that shame, despair, and unspoken struggles permeate our community, deeply affecting all of our sex lives.

With that said, I won't be asking you to love yourself into some kind of new wellness or suggest a sexual life hack. I'm not asking you to be happier or to become a "better" person. What I am asking is that you do for yourself what I've cultivated with the men I've worked with for years: make room for yourself—all of yourself, every last part—even if only for the relatively brief time we'll spend together. As you dive in, I ask that you make an agreement with yourself to stay curious, above all.

While this book is primarily for men who identify as gay, queer, trans, bi, or sexually fluid, and for those who live beyond the gender binary, all are welcome on the journey. Sexual freedom and well-being is the North Star—it's what we move toward by uncovering and exploring our sexual desires, even in the face of unfounded or deeply rooted false beliefs, including the standards our culture imposes on us. It also means exploring those desires alongside our deeply held imprints, anxieties, and insecurities.

The Four Rooms concept comes from an old Indian proverb that likens our whole being to the rooms of a house—separate spaces contained within one structure. The Room of the Mind, the Heart, the Body, and the Spirit. The idea is to visit each room every day, even if only to keep it aired out. The belief is that if we avoid one room while staying safe in another, we limit our experience of wholeness. For the purposes of this book and the work I do, I refer to these Four Rooms as The Room of the Thinking Mind, The Room of the Emotions, The Room of the Sacred, and The Room of the Body.

In the sections of this book that focus on each of these rooms, you'll find some thought experiments and exercises—things to ponder, and if you're inclined, to write or journal about. Ultimately, though, there are no requirements for you to fulfill. I invite you to use this book however it suits you and move through it at whatever pace feels right. The words on these pages are meant to walk alongside you, not lead you. The encouragement and ideas I offer are more about cultivating curiosity and nudging you to become a witness to your own experience, much like I might do if I were in the room with you.

Some who gravitate toward this book may have experienced trauma, abuse, or shame that might surface as they reflect on the topics brought up here. Let me be super clear: I'm *not* asking you to relive your trauma. I'm not asking you to allow overwhelming despair to sit in the room with you as you read this book. I'm also not pushing you into spaces you don't wish to enter. My hope is that this book will reveal parts of you that you may have exiled or haven't yet explored, and to offer a space where you can discover and express yourself— maybe in ways you haven't before.

I have no doubt that your history, traumas, and experiences will come forward. There's no avoiding these things on the path toward greater sexual freedom, but at the same time, there's no need to "accept" or "get over" your issues in order to benefit from this work. That's not what this book is about, and it's not what I'm about, either.

I have my own deep history of trauma, which includes childhood sexual, emotional, and physical abuse, as well as drug addiction, treatment, and recovery in adulthood. As I outlined in my previous book, *Every Grain of Sand*, I know all too well that living in abusive situations, or dealing with mental health struggles and addiction, isn't something a person can realistically overcome just by reading a self-help book.

If you're currently under the care of, or in need of, professional mental health support, I strongly encourage you to make sure you have access to that care before diving into any sensitive, deep work that may arise. I'm excited that you've found this book, and I'm so grateful that you're willing to go on this journey. I just ask that you keep your expectations in check and allow the magic to happen in its own time.

I hope I can help in a variety of ways. I come to you, of course, as a sex work provider, a survivor of childhood abuse, and someone who has experienced long-term recovery—but most importantly, I'm a queer man fully experiencing sexual freedom like never before in my life. While I'm incredibly motivated to share this body of work, I want to be clear that I'm on this journey *with* you. Over the past 18 years, I have jumped in fully and immersed myself in the world of sexuality, love, and intimacy. I want to present some ideas, tools, and maybe a different perspective for those who struggle with sexual freedom. Helping men navigate these choppy waters is my passion, almost by default. In a perfect world, I'd want every man I come into contact with to fall in love with himself and find the kind of sexual freedom he seeks and deserves. Short of that, I want to help as many as I possibly can on this journey.

Reading this book isn't about finding a "better" version of yourself any more than a magnifying glass shows you a "better" image of whatever you're looking at. It might help you clarify and focus on details you hadn't noticed before, but it's simply offering you a new perspective on what's already there. Likewise, I hope this book helps you find a clearer sense of your own truths and who you are, sexually and otherwise. My intention is to challenge you to look inside, outside, and around yourself for the information that's been waiting to be uncovered.

My hope is that the questions I pose will evoke a deeper understanding of what sexual freedom means to *you*—what gets in the way of it, and what you might (or might not) do with that information. This book is about taking sips from the well, not chugging it all at once. It's meant to bring gentle awareness into your life, not earth-shattering change. The idea is to bring ease, not pressure. It doesn't have to be about climbing Mount Everest, resolving every unresolved trauma, or becoming some "better" version of ourselves. How about just being who we are today?

I can tell you from experience that no amount of sexual, physical, or emotional connection with countless men over the years exempts me from the struggles I carry, nor does it insulate me from living under the weight of my own past traumas. I still get nervous sometimes when the clothes come off. Sex can be awkward way more often than you might guess. I still worry about my looks, my arms, my cock—all of it.

Maybe that sounds like bad news to you. I mean, if a veteran sex worker still struggles with this stuff, what possible chance do you have for sexual freedom? At least that's what I imagine going through some of your heads. But from my perspective, that's the good news.

Like any journey, the search for sexual well-being doesn't just happen. It takes intention and motivation to summon the courage to explore and maybe even take some well-calculated risks. As many times as I've cringed reading this statement, I find myself saying it, too: *The fact that you've picked up this book is a great sign.* And by that, I mean it's obvious you've already brought intention into the room. So congratulations. You're here.

Welcome to The Four Rooms.

THE THINKING MIND

I

THE ROOM OF THE THINKING MIND

B eing in my head has always been a struggle. One moment, I'm overanalyzing what might be happening or what just took place. Next, I'm judging myself for overthinking or replaying some past interaction. There's always an inner conversation when I look at my body in the mirror or compare my world to the world of others on social media. Memories—especially of past traumas, triggered by powerful current events—can send me down a rabbit hole of thoughts, ideas, and judgments.

The thoughts that weigh most heavily on my mind are usually the most challenging—*What could I have done differently? What have I done? Why this? Why that? What's it all for anyway?!* As we'll discuss in the next section, these thoughts are often accompanied by a vast spectrum of feelings. There was a time I drank, did drugs, and took medication all in an effort to free myself from the confusion that existed in the clutter and confusion of my constantly thinking mind. I would identify and try to figure out every thought, what it meant, and why I was having it.

I remember when I believed meditation was the answer to all my confusion. I was told—and read in many self-help books—that I should sit in silence, let my thoughts come and go, or count numbers or say mantras to distract my mind. There were times I would sit for hours, struggling with even the most mundane thoughts, because I believed that if I couldn't clear my mind completely, I was "doing it wrong." This is not a critique of the benefits of meditation by any means—I still sit in stillness from time to time, though I don't enjoy it that much. I take downtime and find other ways to meditate. My point is, for many, entering the space of the thinking mind is a confusing endeavor, especially for those of us with loud thoughts that take up more space than they deserve.

The mind is filled with beliefs, judgments, opinions, ideas, and perceptions—not just about ourselves and how we see the world, but also about how we believe the world sees *us*. This section, The Room of the Thinking Mind, is focused on taking stock of those thoughts. Here is where we uncover our imprints and journey toward the roots of our beliefs. Here is where we begin to notice the difference between constructive thinking and self-judgment. Here is where I'll encourage you to get curious.

In the Room of the Thinking Mind, we can begin to witness our thoughts, including the judgments we tend to place on them—or on ourselves, simply for having them. These are the thoughts we often give power to. The ones we might label as negative or self-defeating. The ones that prevent us from being vulnerable and open. It can be a vicious cycle that makes other, more constructive ideas hard to see or allow into the room.

Let me say this now, and I'll probably repeat it: my mission isn't to change your thinking, but to invite you to observe your thoughts, ideas, and beliefs in their natural habitat. One way we can do this is by observing our inner conversations. Doing this without creating a story about what we believe is happening can be challenging. But with time and practice, it gets easier to name what we're thinking and what we observe about our thoughts, ideas, and beliefs.

Becoming the witness rather than the author of some theory or self-assessment about a current circumstance gives us space—it makes the room bigger. Embodying that energy and sense of presence will also bring a bit of peace. Becoming a witness and observer might give us the moment we need to get better at showing up for ourselves, possibly in ways we haven't done in a long time.

You won't need to find a quiet place or sit and ponder your observations, droning through a silent cacophony of invading thoughts. Unless, of course, you want to. As we delve deeper into other, more complicated areas of the thinking mind, this section will present a few tools to foster a less judgmental, less daunting experience in this room, which can often feel messy and confusing.

So buckle up, and let's get started.

FIRST THOUGHTS FIRST

Let's start with the most basic question, even if you don't have the answer right now. Let this be your first brush with some intentional curiosity.

What does sexual freedom look like to you? If you could visualize yourself experiencing sexual freedom and well-being, how would it manifest in your life? Try the closed-eye test. When you think about sexual freedom, what do you see when you close your eyes? What does it look like for you? What's the scene in your imagination? What are you doing?

Sexual freedom means whatever it means—and however many things it means—to each of us individually. You may come up with any number of scenes in your head—romantic, kinky, wild, vanilla. The only limit is your own desire and imagination. Some answers may be foundational and unchanging. Maybe open relationships, polyamory, monogamy, or any other variation is an absolute must in your sex life. Others might reflect a phase you're going through or something you may want today but won't tomorrow. It's as changeable as we are.

There are no rules here. Envision the different ways sexual freedom might manifest in your life. Maybe it brings up thoughts of bathhouses and sex clubs or being part of a queer kink subgroup. Or perhaps you imagine yourself as part of a loving couple, having hot sex on the regular. The examples are endless. The spectrum—from being touched tenderly to being gang-fucked in a bathhouse—is a varied road leading to any number of destinations. The invitation is to use this time to simply notice what feels true for you today.

That might seem obvious, but people withhold the truth from their therapists and doctors all the time—often as a way of withholding it from themselves, avoiding the discomfort it might bring. I don't underestimate that phenomenon. It makes perfect sense that we might go to great lengths to avoid confronting our thoughts and beliefs.

A recurring theme in this book is the absence of definitive right or wrong answers. There's no need to feel boxed in by the questions on these pages. In fact, it's the opposite—this book is your laboratory. Experiment here. As you move through these pages, let this kind of intentional contemplation linger. Don't force anything, but pay attention if you find your mind returning to some of these questions and notice whether your answers evolve over time—or not. Either way, it's all useful information for you.

YOUR IMPRINTS

The idea of imprinting is typically associated with wildlife and human infants, especially in relation to bonding with a parent. However, I've chosen the word *imprinting* because, during our formative years, we bond to certain beliefs and ideas—shaped by religion, media, family, friends, society, culture, peers, and technology. And when I say "formative years," for queer men that can mean any time in our lives, given the varied experiences we have with coming out—or not coming out—and confronting our sexuality, sometimes much earlier or later in life. For queer people, the "typical" adolescent window may not be so predictable.

Are we carrying into the present moment messages informed by the imprints we've picked up in the past? Consider especially the messages from our growing years or from moments when we may have experienced shame, trauma, or abuse. We experience heightened sensitivity to messages in various forms:

Don't be a sissy.

God hates fags.

Sex is shameful.

Taking it up the ass is disgusting.

You don't deserve equal rights.

You're not fit to work with children.

These messages also show up today through societal influences—comments on social media, and commentators on news outlets who spread inflammatory ideas and opinions, especially during times of crisis like the AIDS and COVID-19 pandemics. These moments seem to amplify the rhetoric. Other times, it's centered around legislation, as politicians pit communities against LGBTQIA+2 populations to further their own agendas.

At several points in this book, I'll ask you to reflect on the version of these messages you've carried with you—where they came from and when you first encountered them. I'll inquire about the messages you've received throughout your life about gender, sex, sexuality, love, and intimacy, as well as the beliefs those messages have imprinted on your conscious (and unconscious) mind. Some may feel inescapable, while others might feel less sticky and easier to ignore. You may even discover that what once felt like an imprinted, unchangeable belief is now easy to dislodge and release.

There's a distinct layer of stigma, shame, and difficulty that comes with being queer in this world. It's not just about accepting ourselves or trying to fit into our communities. For some, it's about safety—sometimes even survival. We all know stories of LGBTQIA+2 people who have faced harassment, brutality, and even murder based solely on their sexual identities. For those of us who remember Matthew Shepard's murder, it stands as a symbol of the dangers we face. There are countless stories of brutality, especially toward queer and trans people of color, as well as sex workers who endure unimaginable conditions just to survive.

The laws often favor the attacker over the queer person, sometimes unintentionally influenced by cultural biases and discrimination. Imagine trying to find a jury or community free from homophobic prejudice in places like Kentucky, Florida, Jamaica, or deeply religious countries. These kinds of stories carry a powerful collective message—a message that says loud and clear, "Be afraid, you are unacceptable and deserving of suspicion."

Cultural trauma passed down from generation to generation can also impact our ability to connect with others. This is especially true for men who lived through the AIDS epidemic. That period was marked by unimaginable loss, and for many, it became a reason to withdraw from sex—or at least a source of deep fear around it. Conversely, some men went the opposite direction, becoming much more sexual, despite enduring shame from others and warnings about sexual promiscuity, death, and dying. The stigma and judgment the gay community faced, both internally and from external sources, continue to affect us to this day.

A lot of our sexual trauma is still stuck in 1990. While science has made great strides, many men still live in fear. Even those of us who have evolved and allowed our sexual behavior to flourish still carry the imprint of what happened in the '80s and '90s. And sometimes, that trauma gets passed on to younger generations. Younger generations, who grew up with the internet and have access to so much information—for better or worse—are still saddled with navigating their sexual identities, as much as anyone else.

Gone, however, are the days of living in terror of touching, being touched, and finding spaces to connect. This is great news, and younger people are circling the wagons, supporting one another, and finding ways to be inclusive and welcoming. There's no shortage of sex-positive events, though even these spaces have limitations for some of us who battle every day to live our truth.

Generational experiences vary. Some of us might have had childhoods overshadowed by neglect or abuse. Some of us were taught—directly or indirectly—that sex is shameful and bad. And then there are those who live at the intersection of multiple historically marginalized identities, such as people of color, those who are neurodiverse or live with disabilities, nonbinary and trans people, or members of religious minorities. The farther we are from the dominant paradigm—white, able-bodied, cis male, heterosexual, Christian, American—the more layers of affirmation we may need to find for ourselves. We carry an extra layer of oppression and burden, based on identity alone.

So many queer men are working from a deficit of cultural affirmation. If we were born into a queer identity framed in disempowering and demoralizing terms steeped in shame, how do we begin to reframe it for ourselves? Where is the welcome mat for those coming of age, and how do we reopen closed doors and see beyond the walls we've built?

Even the most well-adjusted queer person carries imprints. It comes with the territory. Those wounds still exist in the recesses of our minds. More importantly, what if that wound or imprint will always be there? We all deal with it differently, no doubt, but one way or another, we *all* deal with it—and probably always will.

We've grown up in a world that tells us that who we are is wrong. Sinful. Unacceptable. That our bodies are unlovable. That our feelings aren't welcome. That who we are has destined us for a lifetime of rejection.

For some of us, this has been the primary experience. For others, it's more in the background. But it's undeniably there—a fact of the world we live in, coloring every area of our lives. Shame, self-loathing, despair, anxiety, and our collective sense of not-enoughness have wreaked havoc on us as individuals and as a broader population of queer men.

From what I've witnessed, it's an epidemic of shame. Each of us experiences some level of internalized homophobia—the stigma that lingers somewhere in our psyches. Even if we've consciously accepted ourselves, many of us still feel a twinge of shame if we do something that fulfills the stereotype we've been told is unacceptable. We might avoid referring to the gender of our partners when chatting with a stranger. We might feel self-loathing after sex. We might cringe at an embarrassing memory.

A lot of queer men will overcompensate their masculinity out of fear of seeming too feminine. Some exaggerate their queerness as a big middle finger to societal shame and those who would limit us. The layers are endless. Not every affect or personality trait is rooted in internal homophobia, but our personalities are undeniably shaped by the environments we grew up in.

When our wound is touched, we might retaliate, lash out, or get angry. Sometimes we shut down, shrink back, or retreat to avoid confronting the feelings that arise. We recoil because there's something beneath the surface—some belief, judgment, or insecurity that's raw, unresolved, and deeper than the incident in question.

Most of us carry some wound or belief that persists into the present, and wherever they manifest, they impact our lives. Though our instinct might be to free ourselves from them, we often shift, maneuver, and try to accept them because it can feel (or at least seem to feel) more comfortable to live with the devil we know than to venture into new territory.

What happens when we seek out information to affirm these beliefs—especially those rooted in shame, fear, or a sense of not-enoughness? We might find ourselves repeating patterns, like hooking up with men who treat us poorly, or relying on the opinions of people with toxic perspectives, like a parent who views us through their own distorted lens. Are we so invested in our own unworthiness that we'll live inside the fortress built from these imprints, rather than face the discomfort of the unknown? Will we choose the comfort of the familiar, even when what's familiar is painful or reflects a sense of emptiness?

I think of imprints as scars on our psyches. Scars are reminders of past wounds, but we often experience them as if they were the original wounds themselves. We might even grow attached to them, believing they're an immutable part of who we are. I have my own share of traumatic imprints, starting with a difficult childhood and adolescence marked by a lot of emotional and physical abuse. I also spent decades in addiction, which led to homelessness, violence, abuse, self-loathing, and despair. It took years of treatment, hospitalizations, institutions, and even imprisonment to recover.

Yet, I've also found success in my chosen endeavors. I've maintained long-term sobriety, do work that I love and am passionate about, and have a wonderful partner of more than twelve years. I now have a kind of confidence I once might have thought impossible to even imagine.

People who meet me might not guess how my history continues to impact me. I love my life, and from the way I live and interact with others, one might assume I'm free from feelings of inadequacy, insecurity, and the like. But guess what? No matter where I've been on this journey, that sense of brokenness, insecurity, word-less anxiety, and fragments of unresolved trauma have resurfaced again and again. Once I stopped trying to get rid of these thoughts and developed a relationship not just with the imprint itself, but also with the feeling of "Oh, I could never, they don't want me around, I'm far too (fill in the blank)," I could better love that part of me as well.

I spent a huge amount of time trying to fix all my broken parts instead of siphoning from their wisdom. Once I was able to see their place in my world, I began to see my whole self more clearly. Warts and all, as they say. There was so much about myself that I was convinced was unacceptable. It took some practice, but learning to step back a bit from that perspective was huge.

So, what do we do with the imprints? How do we deal with a past belief system or trauma that arises when our wounds are touched? What do we do when we feel ashamed and small, and the walls begin to close in on us?

Maybe this leaves you with more questions than answers, and that's OK. You'll come to see that I *like* questions. I know we all want solutions, but the invitation here isn't necessarily about doing nothing—it's about becoming an observer rather than a player in the story.

WHERE'D YOU GET THAT IDEA?

Where do we get these imprints, ideas, and perspectives that keep us locked in illusions of inadequacy? What is the origin story of the belief systems and brilliant strategies that so often steer our lives? Consider how your parents, community, and friends modeled sex, sexuality, and intimacy throughout your life. What messages did you absorb from them? What stories—spoken or unspoken—shaped your understanding of these aspects of yourself?

It's possible—even likely—that we've received mixed messages along the way. I've had lovers who showed me how exciting, hot, and intense sex can be. And I've had others who absolutely mirrored my own feelings of not-enoughness. If you notice mixed messages in your history, recognize that these contradictions are part and parcel of this topic and of being human. Allow these seemingly conflicting messages into the room, along with everything else. They are data. They are information. Be glad for them.

Let's look more closely at the origins of these messages. If you're willing, take a piece of paper and draw two columns. In the left column, make a list of influences: parents, siblings, friends, classmates, contemporaries, society, religious institutions, media and social media, lovers or sex partners, your culture—both queer and societal—and let's not exclude our bullies and abusers. That's a hefty list from which to gather intel.

In the right column, write a few words that capture the story you picked up from those influences. You could uncover a great deal of information through this exercise. Keep in mind, this isn't about implicating guilty parties from our past or pointing fingers at parents or other authority figures. It's about uncovering the memories that sit with you and recognizing how these imprints helped form the foundation of your beliefs.

If we can get curious about the origins of our beliefs, we might better observe their power over us. This won't necessarily make them go away, but it will give us a clearer picture of how they continue to impact us.

Understanding where these beliefs come from inevitably brings up questions about our younger years. Everyone grows up navigating all kinds of stigma around sex. These might include ideas like: being gay is a sin; sex is harmful or dangerous; gay tops are masculine and bottoms are feminine; or what we desire is unacceptable, strange, or abnormal. There's a pervasive stigma in our society that tells queer people they are inherently bad, unacceptable, or flawed simply by virtue of who they were born to be.

Sometimes that stigma limits us from connecting with others, having the sex we desire, enjoying our own bodies, and forming meaningful relationships.

In Arthur Miller's classic play *The Crucible*, the character Elizabeth Proctor tries to explain her distance from her husband over the years. She says, "I counted myself so plain, so poorly made, no honest love could come to me!" Talk about a sense of not being good enough or worthy of love! This is a character identifying with her own imprint, her illusion of inadequacy. Like many brilliant writers, Arthur Miller didn't invent this phenomenon—he saw it as part of the human condition and instilled it into one of his characters. Her feelings are relatable because they are inherently, deeply human.

It's as true for me as it is for you. Old messages still rattle around in my head, trying to take center stage. What if they never truly go away? What if these feelings of insecurity, awkwardness, or fear return, even if they went away for a while? Can we allow insecurity or our imprints to be in the room alongside our desires?

It doesn't take much to touch our wounds and poke our insecurities. A perceived rejection—like someone not responding to a flirtatious signal or ignoring a message on the app—can touch that wound. If we get activated by this, it can feel like confirmation of our worst fears about ourselves.

So why does it sting? Why do we take it so personally? What would it be like to refer to this list of people and influences that have given us more insight? What story on that list confirms my unworthiness? Are there also people on that list who empower and affirm you? We sometimes unwittingly protect ourselves from future harm because of who we think we are and what we think we know—especially what we've come to believe about ourselves as a result of these influences in our lives.

A lot of my own fears and sense of inadequacy are informed by a culture hell-bent on picket fences, heteronormative media, and the constant droning about homosexuality and same-sex relationships being a problem. These messages may have lost some of their power over me, but when I consider this list of influences, what I find is that these imprints are woven into my worldview in ways I may never fully understand—nor do I have to.

What if these ideas-turned-imprints aren't the kind of thing you can simply clear from your memory? Can we get a glimpse of them and see them for what they are? Rather than these external forces being an inherent part of your sexual DNA, maybe they're just road maps inviting us to go deeper and create more space. This isn't a declaration of war—we're not going into battle to stop our insecurity once and for all. This is a peace talk. We invite to the table who you've been told you are and who you think you are, then bring in the mediator—your ever-present inner observer, who allows all the parts of you to be exactly as they are.

Where we got these ideas isn't as important as the relationship we've built with these beliefs. There's a level of dependency and intimacy that comes with being kept safe from our wounds. The idea that we may have to grieve the end of our enmeshment with a core false belief that no longer serves us can be daunting. At the same time—as with all intimate connections—our resilience and ability to coexist with these former guardians of the heart and our deeply held ideas is where the excitement of something new on the horizon lies. We can find freedom in that.

The core of this approach is to notice your thoughts, even if you feel the need to engage with them. Let them sit with you as you notice patterns of evaluation, problem-solving, and self-judgment. Get curious about the ways your thoughts and beliefs might limit your sexual freedom. Who do you tell yourself you are, and how might those messages act as obstacles to the kind of sex life and sexual freedom you envision for yourself?

Our beliefs about our identity—especially those born from trauma or rebellion—play a crucial role in our capacity to connect intimately with others, sexually or otherwise. What kind of self-talk happens when you get timid in the face of a sexual opportunity? Are we prone to unkind, knee-jerk self-assessments?

The question is, what happens beyond that internal hellscape of fear? Could it be an easy out, a chance to bypass the pain of our illusion? Could it be an effort to protect ourselves from being rejected or reminded that we're not lovable? Could this be why we create stories like "I'm too old to enter into a relationship," "I'm too fat, and nobody wants a fat guy," "My cock is too small," "I don't need anybody. I can take care of myself," or "Why bother? It'll just create more stress."

The list goes on. Many of us have no trouble naming all kinds of ways in which we feel unworthy. And that's just what we're consciously aware of. There's a whole realm of unconscious beliefs and biases we live by without even realizing it.

Once our ideas, thoughts, judgments, and opinions about ourselves, others, or the experience we're having begin to emerge alongside feelings like disappointment and shame, the illusion of inadequacy can—and most often will—take root. That's when we once again find ourselves with our shields up, isolating, drinking too much, or back on the therapist's couch.

We continue affirming "the problem." These moments, over time, make it less likely that we'll risk putting ourselves out there again, creating a self-perpetuating cycle. As an aside, let's not forget the couple who's been together for many years. Sexual intimacy has waned, companionship has weakened, and communication has become difficult—all born from the fear of disappointing each other, fear of expressing desires, or feeling ashamed. They're lost in their own version of communication paralysis. Their desires are so enmeshed, they're so familiar with each other, that shaking up the ship feels uncomfortable and destabilizing. The good news is, there's love and history there, so these relationships require courage and inquiry to grow together—each doing their own work as well.

THE PROBLEM WITH THE PROBLEM

What if your problem—whatever it is that keeps you from the kind of sexual freedom you want—weren't, in fact, a problem? I'm talking about feeling unattractive, not well-endowed enough, not confident enough, or whatever else it might be. What if that were simply data you're working with, independent of the challenges it presents? What if it were information—a tool—you could use? That might sound simplistic. I'm not dismissing our issues but suggesting we stay open to the possibility that we can see our so-called problems in a constructive way. The goal of this book isn't to "fix" you or solve any specific problems. Rather, it's an invitation to explore your whole sexual well-being.

For many (maybe even most) of us, it's human nature to see our challenges as problems to be solved. Our entire culture is steeped in problem-solving. From our earliest days, we've been taught that if we solve a problem, we'll be rewarded. Give the right answer in school, and you get that gold star of approval. Similarly, in our lives as sexual beings, finding someone to have sex with is so often framed as a conquest—something we either succeed or fail at.

But what if the problem with the problem is that we keep trying to solve the problem?

I often refer to this project as a non-self-help book, and here's why. The premise isn't to solve your problems, but to cultivate curiosity around your relationship to the idea of the problem. We tend to think that our imprints are the problem, whether they're subtle or glaring. These deeply held ideas and beliefs can magnify our sense of being unacceptable and unlovable. Some of the hardest imprints to ignore are the ones that reinforce our feelings of not-enoughness. These imprints are insidious because we want to get rid of them—these memory-like beliefs about ourselves and the world we live in. We try to push them away or ignore them. We may build resistance or seek mountains of therapeutic remedies, all in an effort to quell the imprint—or, in other words, "to solve the problem."

The practice of finding freedom from the problem can also deprive us of sitting with the wisdom the so-called problem brings. It's an invitation to go deeper and explore other possibilities without waving a white flag of surrender. This doesn't mean your struggles don't exist. It means we get to focus on noticing and allowing them to be in the room, along with other information, without trying to fix anything. The power lies in staying curious rather than seeking a solution.

All too often, we're surrounded by unrealistic standards. We easily get caught up in measuring what we think we're supposed to be or in how happy, well-adjusted, or sexually free everyone else seems compared to where we think we are in different areas of our lives. Social media comes to mind here. We spend too much time comparing our insides to other people's outsides. Instagram is filled with well-polished photos and lifestyle ideas, full of unfair comparisons we can never hope to live up to. One of my friends calls Facebook "Put-on-your-best-face-book."

A primary obstacle to sexual freedom is our personal sense of not-enoughness. While "enoughness" may not be a word, as a concept, it's at the heart of why I do this work. The feelings of inadequacy, the doubts, the fears, and the perceived problems we carry make the rooms we dwell in feel smaller because we're only seeing part of the larger picture. The shadow cast by these feelings can obscure or block our sense of what we're doing well, the assets we bring to the table, and the possibilities for sexual fulfillment.

When we get curious about what else is possible, the room feels more expansive. This gives us the grace to discover that many of our long-held notions about where we fall short or how we won't "get it right" are often filled with information about ourselves, offering a perspective with less self-judgment. Then it becomes possible to own our beliefs from a wider angle, allowing ourselves to embody much more than the narrow view of "I am not enough" or any other "I am" statement we apply to ourselves.

FITTING IN ISN'T BELONGING

One thing I've noticed from my own experience of "not-enoughness" is that I often tried to fit in rather than truly belong. I explored new friend groups, joined clubs, and became part of various communities. I benefited greatly from these experiences and learned a lot about myself.

When I felt like I didn't belong to a certain community or stopped attending an event they hosted, I began to question my motives. Along with my doubts came the fear that I wasn't wanted or liked by its members. Secretly, in the back of my mind, I imagined they saw me as an outsider.

It blew my mind wide open when I came across a short video of Brené Brown in an interview with Lewis Howes. During their discussion on belonging, she said, "I was so shocked to learn in the research that the opposite of belonging is fitting in. Because fitting in is assessing a group of people and thinking, who do I need to be? What do I need to say? What do I need to wear? How do I need to act? And changing who you are. And true belonging never asks us to change who we are. It demands that we 'be' who we are."

My trying to fit in, instead of feeling my own sense of belonging, actually did make me an outsider in my own world—locked in the belief that I didn't fit in, when what I truly wanted was to belong.

In our exploration of belonging, we might experiment with subgroups or try new activities. Maybe you want to throw on some leather gear and head to a kinky leather event, or you might join a speed-dating group. Some have joined puppy groups, a subculture mostly made up of younger, gregarious queer people who get together for all sorts of things, with sexual frivolity being just one of them. Pups are incredibly visible in the kink community, often doing service projects and hosting inclusive events that are broad in their reach.

While certainly not required, most puppies will don a mask, sometimes even a tail. It's a social experience for most of them. Seeing the playful connectedness and loyalty they share can be very attractive to someone seeking a sense of belonging. There are handlers and a variety of roles to explore. Jumping in, of course, is fantastic and adventurous fun. I love the pups!

But at what point does exploration intersect with the desire to belong, and when does it become an attempt to fit in? Are we becoming something other than who we are in an effort to seek approval and validation? Does integrating ourselves into subgroups in order to feel connected actually serve us? Maybe it does—sometimes it leads to incredible discoveries. Validation is affirming, especially in subcultures and communities where many explorers have existed on the margins.

True connection is powerful, but sometimes we change who we are out of fear of not belonging. The cautionary tale here is to be mindful of the times we take risks or let our boundaries be crossed for fear of being cast out or rejected. We may stumble into experiences that don't align with our personal values. Then there's the peer pressure to partake in recreational drugs, which, in and of itself, may not be a concern—until excessive or addictive use leads to complications and consequences, both internal and external. We can get comfortable betraying ourselves when we weigh it against the fear of being alone. Many people who emerge from isolation and disconnection into a sense of belonging—even if it's inauthentic—might think, "At least I'm not locked away in my room, filled with dread and depression." Then, boom! We party till we're homeless, or worse.

What I'm trying to express is the importance of noticing whether we're changing who we are just to feel like we belong—and what gets created when we present an edited or smaller version of ourselves just to sit at the group's table. Just some food for thought.

I AM MORE THAN MY NAME TAG

Name tags—we all wear them. Some obvious ones might be, "Hello, I'm David. I'm gay, queer, left-handed, a Virgo, versatile, and sober." But we also wear other proverbial name tags, ones that go beyond a simple "I am" statement, shaped by imprints we've carried for so long that we feel defined by them. We often feed on a mental diet of junk thoughts—perceptions about not being enough, or that something in the world is not enough. Just like you are what you eat, what if you are what you think? So, what are you feeding your psyche, and what are the results?

What are your "I am" statements? They might sound like "I am too fat," "I am so stupid," "I am too old," or "I am too skinny." We also create statements that impact how we view the world, like "My dick isn't big enough" or "Nobody will date a guy like me." What happens when we decide something is true for us and begin to "wear" that truth like a name tag? Some of these name tags provide intel about where we believe we fit in or what subculture we identify with. Once we declare that we're a particular thing or that the world is a certain way, it becomes hard to stay flexible.

When we've committed to a certain label—"I am unacceptable," "I am insecure," "I don't drink, and the bars are full of alcoholics," "I have anxiety so I can't deal with dating," and so on—we end up writing rules for ourselves that we're hesitant to break. What set of rules must we follow to keep our name tags intact?

For instance, consider someone who identifies as demisexual because they have a real need for connection before having sex. Fair enough, but what comes along with that name tag? Do they develop opinions and judgments to accompany this identity? Consider declarations like:

"I don't go to sex parties—I can't connect in a crowd."

"I'm all about monogamy, so I won't use the apps, nor will I date men that do."

As a sex worker, I saw a wide variety of name tags. Name tags can be sexually affirming—it's empowering to know and own your desires. The question is, does this name tag include judgments about ourselves or others? Do they serve to keep us separate? Our name tags can create a sense of not belonging anywhere that the name tag doesn't apply.

I often hear statements like "I'm not into hookup culture," "I need to connect and know someone first," or "Gay cruises are floating bathhouses. I can't go on them—everyone is high on drugs, and that's not my scene." These sound like rules and boundaries based on preconceived notions or past experiences, and they play right into the name tag we wear.

I've been on more than twenty-five gay cruises, and I have more than eighteen years of sobriety. I also met my partner of more than twelve years on a gay cruise. I know for a fact there's something for a lot of people on these cruises. Many don't drink or do drugs, while some love to. Some don't hook up, and some play and have sex with everyone they can. Some meet, fall in love, and have a great time. Others go just to enjoy the entertainment and the ambience and to be surrounded by their community in a big gay floating bubble. This is just one example of how our name tags create ideas and opinions. Maybe you can come up with some of your own.

The concept of name tagging feels particularly relevant in the LGBTQIA+2+ community, where we constantly attach identities to ourselves—top, bottom, submissive, dominant, master, slave, bear, twink, and so on. But just because we tag ourselves this way doesn't mean we won't run into experiences that challenge these identities. The question then becomes, can we stay flexible enough to try something new or step outside the usual experience? Or do we shut ourselves off from these possibilities because of something we've attached to our name tag? There's a bit of social pressure in the queer community to live up to your name tag, play your part, and stick to your role. We fear what might happen if we diverge from that role. Does it make me dishonest, a fraud, an imposter? Will I no longer belong or fit in?

From a professional standpoint, sex workers experience this pressure because we want to attract guys who are into our brand—like being seen as a "total top." Then we make a video where we're more versatile or just bottoming. You might think that would mean more business. Not always. There's so much stigma, shame, and judgment around bottoming or being more submissive that many of these men don't want to be flexible. They've name-tagged you as the dominant guy, the one in control, which sets expectations and provides a sense of safety. Because of their unwillingness to explore beyond their internal biases, they'll only hire guys who fit exactly into their scope of desire. It's a choice and a valid one—it's their money, and they get to decide how to spend it. But it's a clear example of how we can limit our possibilities when we remain rigid or stuck behind a name tag. Once we've attached our name tag and identified with it deeply, it can be hard to change or remove it.

The Room of the Thinking Mind is a place to witness our thoughts and beliefs. We can do the same for our name tags—evaluating these beliefs about ourselves without labeling them as right, wrong, good, or bad. What would it be like to let the room have more than just the name tag? What would it be like to ask questions like, "What else is possible here?" or "What's working that I'm not seeing?" We can acknowledge that labels aren't necessarily inaccurate but are merely surface-level—a kind of shorthand, rather than a corner we paint ourselves into.

What if we also released our expectations, opinions, and judgments about others who wear name tags different from ours? Can we offer them the same flexibility we offer ourselves? When we hold too tightly to our ideas of who we think we are—and who we think others are—we close the room.

The Room of the Thinking Mind has as much capacity for expansion as it does for contraction. The good news is, we get to ask ourselves an important question: What if I'm more than my name tag?

WHO ELSE IS POSSIBLE?

So far, we've briefly uncovered what's been stopping us from fully being who we are and how we limit our sexual expression in an attempt to protect ourselves from being wounded. We've talked about what else is possible beyond operating from a fear of rejection or the belief that we're unacceptable as we are. We've pondered the possibility that we're much more than our name tags.

As we explore the reasons we keep ourselves behind protective walls, I want to present another way to cultivate curiosity. We're often quick to explain why we respond the way we do when experiences push our triggers. We may even identify with a diagnosis of depression or anxiety, or point to a past traumatic experience. These are perfectly valid reasons for why we react the way we do, especially when we're about to get naked—emotionally or physically. But allow me to pose another question that may be helpful as we explore sexual freedom and well-being in the context of this work:

Who else is possible here?

What part of you have you not allowed to show up? What version of yourself have you exiled to be more acceptable or to fit in? When I refer to "who else is possible here," that's exactly what I mean. It's an invitation to discover parts of you that you may not have noticed or have yet to uncover. There could be a part of you that you've lost sight of.

Sometimes we don't access certain parts of ourselves as much as we'd like. We focus on who we think we are and how we think the world sees us, rather than exploring who else might be possible in this moment. You don't even need to know this aspect of yourself yet. Simply asking the question can allow something new to emerge. It's an exercise to replace thoughts like "Why am I like this?" or "What the fuck is wrong with me?"— questions that disempower us and are too common in a culture obsessed with solving problems.

When we get curious—and I'm going to encourage us to get curious a lot—this is one of the questions that will come in handy. It's as if we have an internal committee of sorts that can veto our need to hide or play small. The voting majority doesn't always get the final say. I encourage inner debate and dialogue, especially with the parts of us that aren't often heard. That's how we make the room more expansive and inclusive. Maybe there are other internal voices waiting to be heard. The key is to pay attention and listen with wonder and compassion, rather than with the urge to resolve our feelings of not-enoughness, our anxieties, or any other conglomerate of problems waiting to be fixed.

Asking "who else is possible here" is another tool—a moment to pause, then keep moving. The answer may or may not arrive as some sudden superpower or in a clearly defined version of yourself that can waltz into the party and be the belle of the ball. But just the act of being curious and allowing ourselves not to attach to a specific reason for our paralysis could be enough to step back and catch our breath. So, in moments of confusion, uncertainty, or when your wound is touched, seek other options by asking yourself, "Who else is possible here?"

WAYNE'S STORY

In the developing stages of this work, I created The Four Rooms workshop, with barely an outline in hand. I hosted a men's retreat at my house over Mother's Day weekend in 2021, with twelve incredible men. At one point, I was having a conversation with a participant named Wayne, a gay man in his forties, married to his partner in an open relationship of many years. We were reviewing an exercise called "Who do you think you are," which focused on our core limiting beliefs.

"I'm too inexperienced with sex," Wayne said, reading from a worksheet he'd completed. "Now it's too late. I held off for too long, and now I'll never feel comfortable. I'm too old to date, too out of shape, and I have no idea what to do when I'm with guys. I can't even imagine that they might be into me at all. Besides that, what does my husband see in me anyway?"

It was nothing I hadn't heard before. In fact, I hear this from the men I work with all the time. My lofty goal with the exercise was to help Wayne see the difference between what he was telling himself and what was really true.

As he continued, I kept circling back to one question: "What's really true here?" I figured if I could just get Wayne to see the truth, then he'd automatically be a step closer to the sexual freedom he was looking for. I had all kinds of ideas about how everything would fall into place for him once he did.

As it turned out, I was very mistaken.

While Wayne talked about how it was too late for him and how nobody could possibly want him sexually, I kept trying to get him to change his view. But every time I offered a thought or suggestion, he found a way to shut the door on it. I assumed he was avoiding the conclusion I wanted him to reach—that he was bullshitting himself right out of a fulfilling sex life, one false belief at a time.

Then Wayne said something that punched me in the gut.

"I know it's not true," he said. "But it feels like a part of me."

Wayne was so committed to his imprint, so invested in his name tag, that it was impossible for him to see anything else, even though he knew he was operating from falsehoods. In an unconscious way, he'd come to see his own imprint—a sense of absolute inadequacy—as an integral part of himself. Even though he could clearly see and understand what was showing up, his strategy was to use his core false beliefs as a shield. From my point of view, his unconscious way of protecting his heart was by remaining unloved and unacceptable. It may sound irrational, but it's not so unusual. Living under the sway of our imprints is an incredibly human thing to do.

If I asked you to think more closely about your own limiting beliefs, you could probably identify one or more as some kind of bullshit you were told, taught, or that you tell yourself—or all of the above. Wherever it came from, and no matter how obviously untrue it might be, it's still a false belief you live by. It's similar to superstition, which doesn't need to be grounded in reality to hold power over us.

I'm not super interested in the content of any individual's imprints. What interests me—and where I hope I can be of service—is discovering how we've bonded with these imprints and our sense of not-enoughness. I wish I'd known enough not to try ridding Wayne of his low self-esteem and instead focused on broadening his perspective. If I could redo that session, I wouldn't try to talk him out of his beliefs, but rather help him see they were only part of the picture. Instead of asking him, "What's really true?" I'd have spent more time asking, "What else is possible?" or "Who else is possible?"

Wayne was so committed to his belief—"It's too late for me. I'm completely dysfunctional"—that he forgot other possibilities existed. This might not sound like much, but it's the difference between "It's too late for me. I'm never going to be good enough," and "I have this fear that it's too late for me and that I'm never going to be good enough."

A big distinction here—the only fact in that moment during the workshop was the latter: "I'm afraid it's too late for me." Wayne's fear was a fact, and it's one I wouldn't try to talk him out of, even if I could have that conversation to do over again.

THE BS FACTOR

My mentor TJ Woodward once posed a seemingly easy question. "David," he asked, "do you know what BS stands for?"

I answered as you probably would have. "Bullshit," I said.

Then he replied, "Did you know it also stands for 'belief system?'"

In other words, the bullshit we tell ourselves can easily evolve into "facts" if we allow them to. It was an aha moment for me, but he wasn't done. He named a third meaning for BS, which was "brilliant strategy," referring to the ways we learn to survive when we feel unsafe, usually from an early age. In this conversation, we were talking about addictions, but it drove home something deeper for me. Ever since that day, I've thought about BS as having not one but three meanings: Bullshit, Belief System, and Brilliant Strategy.

BULLSHIT refers to false beliefs or imprints that lack a factual or rational basis. For example: "I'm an unlovable person." I mean, maybe some people are unlovable, but in all likelihood, this is the kind of thing too many of us tell ourselves all the time—and it's bullshit.

By identifying bullshit for what it is, we open ourselves up to more honest and informed perspectives. And by seeing how else our BS operates, we can add context to it without having to completely shed it. "I am too fat." You might be unhappy with your weight, but this statement falls under the bullshit definition because it blocks you from feeling acceptable. There's nothing unusual about being unhappy with your size, but that doesn't make you unacceptable—for proof, just look at the thriving bear community.

In what ways do our bullshit ideas and unloving beliefs about ourselves serve us? If we didn't benefit—either consciously or unconsciously—from our bullshit, we probably wouldn't lean into it so often.

BELIEF SYSTEMS are deeply ingrained beliefs or imprints that form a framework or code of conduct for how we live. They can be passed down through generations, from family units to broader cultural experiences. Belief systems can sometimes be steeped in dogma, religious tenets, and cultural standards or expectations.

What comes to mind when we think of our personal belief systems? Whether or not they're grounded in reality, these beliefs often guide our values and morals and shape our judgments. We might have been brought up in a family that believed being gay is a sin, or that marriage is only between a man and a woman, with the motto "love the sinner, hate the sin."

These belief systems profoundly shape one's worldview and can lead to feeling obligated to remain tied to the beliefs we grew up with. We might even be convinced we must care for a parent who was or is abusive, manifesting a tendency to take care of others or stay in unhealthy relationships because that's what we saw modeled growing up. We can feel like we are a disappointment if our values don't align with those we were raised with. Excavating the guilt buried beneath these layers is quite a journey.

Belief systems are complex. Even if they don't make sense to others, we hold on to them deeply because they feel like a part of us. They're something we've always known to be true. Family systems often pass down most of our belief systems, though they can also inspire rebellious, contrary belief systems. We might, for instance, form ideas in opposition to what we were taught growing up. Maybe we had a parent who struggled with alcohol addiction, so now we don't drink. There are many layers to belief systems—some are adapted, while others feel absolute. All are woven into our worldview and can be incredibly powerful.

BRILLIANT STRATEGIES are the beliefs we develop and actions we take to safeguard ourselves emotionally, mentally, or physically. These strategies—often called coping mechanisms—arise in direct response to the bullshit we tell ourselves and the belief systems we grew up with. We might have used drugs, alcohol, sex, or shopping as a strategy to avoid feeling our feelings. Sometimes our emotions were so big, insurmountable, and unbearable that we relied on brilliant strategies to change our experience and protect ourselves. Even though they may be based on bullshit, brilliant strategies are aptly named because, on some level, they do protect us, even if under false pretenses.

Imagine someone saying, "Everyone deserves to be in a relationship, so where is my partner?" (belief system). "I must be an unlovable person. Nobody wants someone like me" (bullshit). "That's why I don't go to bars anymore—who needs that much rejection?" (brilliant strategy).

Put another way: Bullshit is the message. Belief system is what informs the message. Brilliant strategy is the action (or inaction) we take as a result. They all come into play and intersect with each other, but in the Room of the Thinking Mind, we make room for all of it.

What I learned when Wayne acknowledged his bullshit was that he was operating on partial information and focusing on a narrow possibility: "I'll never meet anyone who really wants me." He knew that wasn't the only possible reality, but he was giving it credence as if it were. He hadn't just bought into the bullshit as fact—he'd allowed this "fact" to block his view of any other path or possible outcome, even though his conscious mind, when pressed, could logically see that other possibilities existed.

If all he had to work with was a belief system ("Nobody wants to date a guy that's out of shape"), then the bullshit belief that followed ("It's too late for me") and the brilliant strategy that kept him safe from future hurt ("I'm not going to try anymore") would be supported by 100 percent of the "evidence" on the table. I see this happen quite a bit.

Wayne's story struck a chord with me. What if we developed an intimate connection to our imprints and bonded to them? What if, long ago, we created a relationship with them that feels like it's serving us, even though some parts of our imprints are actually holding us back? I doubt this is intentional—it's likely instinctual. It's probably how we develop brilliant strategies in the first place. This realization sent me into my studio in a flurry to write it down, helping me unlock one of the foundational questions of this work: "What if our imprints belong to us, and they are a sacred part of our whole being?"

After my retreat, I started thinking more about self-improvement and the personal growth industry as a whole. It feels like a perfect example of how we get stuck on the treadmill of problem-solving. We keep trying to change ourselves because we believe there's some part of us that's unwanted, unacceptable, or unlovable. We often think that if we can just remove what we believe is "bad," or take a personal growth course, or do an ayahuasca ceremony, we'll be free from our challenges once and for all.

The self-improvement industry thrives on convincing us that our problems need to be solved. That's why our imprints and deeply held beliefs about what is "wrong" with us are so hard to navigate. What if we saw our imprints, our beliefs, and even our flaws as sacred and important parts of us, even if they're difficult and scary?

Our imprints can be invitations if we allow them to be. They contain a lifetime of wisdom and information about how we experience the world we live in. The room is far bigger than we think, and if we pull the camera back a bit to see the full scope of our situation, we might notice there's much more to the story. If there's wisdom in the shadowy parts of us that hold us back, then were we really being held back—or just on pause until we found enough space to release the grip on what might be blocking us from seeing the rest of the room?

LIVING IN THE QUESTIONS

In the context of The Four Rooms, "living in the questions" is an exercise in cultivating curiosity. If you haven't already noticed, this book is driven largely by inquiry, curiosity, and questions. Living in the questions can be incredibly useful when it comes to self-observation. When we're less busy deciding what something means, or what its value is or isn't, something else can fill that space instead.

What happens when we stay curious, instead of labeling something as "bad" and running away from it? We can get curious and introspective about our experiences with sex, love, and intimacy—but it takes practice. If we don't work that muscle, we become prone to atrophy and sluggishness. Our motivation for a better sexual adventure begins to wane. So let's put in the work.

What if our imprints, limiting beliefs, and various forms of BS are invitations to further inquiry rather than shackles on our sexual freedom? Our sense of not being enough can inspire more questions: What if I am enough? What parts of me already are enough? You can try this exercise with anything else that comes up. For example, when we react to social issues, bad actors, or other frustrations, these moments offer great opportunities to practice living in the questions.

This practice of cultivating curiosity toward our own imprints, limiting beliefs, and the things we tell ourselves about our relationship to sex, love, and intimacy can be incredibly freeing. This is where we can introduce question marks alongside all those declarative statements your thinking mind pumps out daily. If you're experiencing a debilitating or limiting inner dialogue, then let's deepen the conversation. Part of being a good conversationalist—even with yourself—is asking more empowering questions.

This tool invites us to shift from how certain we are about our limitations into a more inquiry-driven, empowering dialogue. It takes practice, especially if you've spent your entire life under the sway of your imprints, beliefs, and ideas about yourself.

But let me underscore this as strongly as I can: Answers are not the goal here.

I mentioned earlier how our human nature leans heavily toward identifying and solving problems. We tend to treat our emotional and sexual lives the same way. But for now—for today, right here, as you work through this book—let me invite you to call off the search for answers and focus on the search for empowering questions. With a bit of time and intention, this shift toward curiosity—turning our limiting beliefs into questions that broaden the conversation—will start to feel more natural, and over time, perhaps even instinctive.

That's when the empowering questions start to arrive more readily. They don't necessarily free us from the paralyzing self-talk that reinforces the preconceptions we carry, but they do add another voice to the conversation. And broadening our focus in this way is one of the key tools for this work.

Here are a few examples, but these are by no means something you need to figure out or "get right." The point is to explore how this inquiry makes you feel. Are you curious and encouraged by being open to more possibilities, or does the question you ask slam down a disgruntled answer? Either way, you get to drive the conversation.

Disempowering Belief: "I can't have sex without being high."
Empowering Question: "What would it feel like to have incredible sex without being high?"

Disempowering Belief: "I'm unattractive and undesirable. I don't look like those guys on Instagram."
Empowering Question: "What would it be like to feel confident and desirable? What is it like to feel beautiful on a deeper level? What if I am actually desirable?"

Disempowering Belief: "I'm too afraid to ask for what I want because I fear rejection."
Empowering Question: "What would it be like if I asked for what I want despite my fears?"

Disempowering Belief: "I'm too self-conscious and insecure to enjoy sex. Nobody wants to fuck me. I'm too fat."

Empowering Question: "How would it feel to embrace my body as is? What if I were fuckable at any size? How does it feel to see myself as completely acceptable?"

What is a limiting, disempowering, or bullshit belief you carry with you? And how might you accompany that thought with a more empowering point of inquiry? Try to make a habit of this for a few days. See where it leads you. Whenever disempowering self-talk arises, reimagine it as an empowering question.

Over time, make a conscious habit of it. This kind of curiosity can be powerful. Curiosity and inquiry are probably the most potent tools this book has to offer. The next time you're mentally beating yourself up over something, take a minute and add a few questions to the declarative statements running through your head.

Those limiting beliefs are not your boss. They are, in fact, a sacred part of you. So consider making room for them and allowing them, then begin an inquiry about what else might be possible here.

THE PRACTICE OF ALLOWING

I feel compelled to hammer down a bit more on what exactly I'm employing here in the Room of the Thinking Mind. Living in the questions is an invitation to ask empowering questions in the face of a wound, an imprint, or unloving self-talk.

The practice of *allowing* is the second part of living in the questions. It's the practice of moving beyond the need to change your opinion or belief and letting go of the idea that some outcome needs to transpire.

The challenge here is to allow your inquiry to remain unresolved and your judgment to remain unencumbered by the desire to change it. The practice of allowing is, in fact, allowing yourself to be exactly who you are in that moment while cultivating curiosity.

At the risk of minimizing the importance of this idea and this tool, I want to give an example of this in action. I use this example because it would be a pretty big stretch to expect anyone to just "get the gist of this" when it comes to all things sex, love, and intimacy, so I'll use a nonsexual example.

Imagine a speeding car cutting us off and then running a red light. When we witness this, stress chemicals shoot through our brain. We immediately honk our horn and yell at the windshield. From inside our car, there's little else we can do about what happened. We take a breath and let it go, grumbling about how nobody knows how to drive these days.

As we continue along, we pass a hospital and see the driver jump out of his car and run into the emergency room in a panic.

We're in a position of discovery, a rare opportunity to find out why something that created a reaction from us happened. The trick is to be on the lookout for other possible reasons, ideas, and outcomes without having to know. Allow what is to be what is, while simultaneously being in inquiry about what else is possible. We can scream at the driver from inside our car while at the same time allowing ourselves to be curious. Those fuckers! Wow, they're in a hurry—I wonder what's happening?

This anecdote shines a light on how "allowing" works. When we allow ourselves to ask empowering questions rather than make judgments of what is happening, we allow other possibilities to arise. Living in the questions is one of the methods of making the room bigger and more expansive.

The Room of the Thinking Mind is the messiest room in the house. I'm not here to shut down the brain or to say that thoughts won't arise. As a matter of fact, I say allow them all, then get curious. Ask a few questions about those thoughts, beliefs, and ideas. Why not? Using the tools of living in the questions and the practice of allowing, I have become a witness to my thoughts, imprints, and ideas of not-enoughness.

As I said earlier, it does take some practice. It's almost like learning to think in a different language. I will caution once again: It can be challenging if we think we're here to solve our problems, change who we are, or stop our thoughts and ideas about our self-worth from arising.

The Room of the Thinking Mind is powerful. Your relationship to your beliefs is your own, and they are sacred and important. Gather wisdom from every single one that arrives. When we live in the ideas of possibility and allowing, we more easily cultivate curiosity around our sexual well-being. Finally, I want to acknowledge that I've never, in well over fifty years of living, been able to master my thoughts. I'll leave that to the Jedi. Once I stopped trying to change my thoughts, however, the battle was over, and the adventure began.

SEXUAL AWARENESS IN *QUEER*Y

Take a moment to reflect on your sex life in light of the Room of the Thinking Mind. This is not about making changes but about becoming more aware. If you like, use a journal to capture any thoughts that arise.

Reflect on the last time you engaged in sexual pleasure. This could include self-pleasure, a hookup, cruising on the street, a scheduled sex-work appointment (massage, escort, live cam show, etc.), online sexting, or sex with a partner.

What stands out about this experience? Do you remember what you were thinking? Were you fantasizing, checking out, being in the moment, engaging in critical self-talk, or considering it an act of self-care? It's OK if you can't remember the details.

Do you have a favorite way to get off, such as watching porn, fantasizing, using toys, getting blow jobs, jacking off, or getting penetrated? Do you hold any judgment or beliefs about your preferences?

Throughout your day and the week ahead, remember to practice asking empowering questions—and to live in those questions rather than try to answer them. Allow ideas and answers to arrive on their own. Your role is simply to observe and gather insights you can use.

THE EMOTIONS

II

THE ROOM OF THE EMOTIONS

For as long as I can remember, I've struggled to control my emotions. I was often told they were out of control, that how I expressed them wasn't okay, and that I was overreacting. I admit I was—and still am sometimes highly sensitive. I grew up feeling unsafe—constantly on edge, fearing belittlement, violence, and humiliation. Sometimes, I was so afraid that I would scream for help one moment, then retreat into silent submission the next. I spent much of my life trying to mask my emotions. I built a wall around them and made careful, deliberate choices about when, where, and to whom I would express them.

I was never stoic or reserved, but my emotions didn't align with healthy self-expression. I learned to play roles, to be whatever version of myself was needed to survive. As an adult, after a great deal of work, I slowly began to find my voice and tune in to my truth. Over time, I learned to express my emotions in ways that felt more true to who I am. I'm no master of self-control, but I no longer see my anger, shame, or despair as something to be hidden or avoided. I now view my emotions as sacred and welcome.

Do I like them all the time? No. Do I resist them? Yes, almost always—at least at first, until I can make enough room for them. I have to remind myself that even the emotions I dread carry wisdom. I spent years chasing happiness, believing it was the answer. And honestly I was mostly just trying to find peace. I tried all the self-help strategies: affirmations, breathwork, meditation, even medication. A big part of my addiction was about changing how I felt because, for a long time, I just couldn't live in my own skin.

Sex was easy for me. I could engage in it for a long time because, at one point, I believed it was just sex—no connection, often about survival. But things changed when I began having intimate, loving relationships. I had to connect honestly and fully with the men I worked with and the men I dated. That's when all my fears, emotions, and baggage came to the surface. My defenses went up, and I was ready to fight—or run. Running was a big one for me. It used to be nothing for me to pack up and walk away from relationships because I couldn't be vulnerable or honest.

Even with the men I worked with early on, I was learning. It took me a while, and I think a lot has come up for me even while writing this book. It took years to finish because I'd take long breaks to work through whatever emotional barriers were holding me back. So, I take this section very seriously. I write it with care and with the understanding that feelings can be overwhelming and confusing. Sometimes, we don't even know what we're feeling—we just know we're uncomfortable and in resistance. Believe me, I get it.

I can still be very sensitive and easily swept up in my emotions at any moment. Much of what follows focuses on the feelings that come up as we explore the journey toward sexual freedom and well-being. We'll explore how issues like shame, fear, people-pleasing, minimizing ourselves, and the compulsion to ensure everyone else's comfort can disrupt our emotional equilibrium. We'll also raise our awareness of these inner processes to counterbalance the powerful hold these emotions can have on us.

I truly believe that for us to flourish in our sexual, loving, and intimate lives—our connection with others and ourselves—this emotional work is often the most complicated. We may think it's all about love, until we realize that our shadowy parts are important markers on the road map toward it.

We've laid the groundwork in the Room of the Thinking Mind, focusing on witnessing our thoughts and beliefs without judgment. Now, I ask you to bring that same approach to your emotions. The Room of the Emotions can sometimes feel like a storage unit full of pain, confusion, despair, and loneliness. We might encounter unpleasant feelings tied to our illusions of inadequacy or not being enough. Notice them, and then notice any resistance you might feel toward certain emotions.

We won't describe emotions as good or bad, right or wrong—they're simply information. You may catch yourself judging some of the feelings that come up, and that's OK. We can still journey toward sexual freedom without judging ourselves for trying to push certain emotions away. Just as with the Room of the Thinking Mind, notice when this happens and see it as one part of a bigger picture.

In the Room of the Thinking Mind, I invited you to allow all the thoughts, ideas, and judgments that arose. In my experience, our thoughts are much more difficult—if not impossible—to control or change. In the Room of the Emotions, however, I invite a bit more flexibility. We don't need to conjure up emotions that might lead us to re-experience trauma or anxiety. Some feelings can be incredibly overwhelming, and we may have developed strategies to avoid our most difficult emotions. If you're experiencing something too uncomfortable or destabilizing, I encourage you to lean on those strategies and your support systems to help you navigate those emotions.

WHAT HAPPENS IN THE ROOM

For the most part, the men I have worked with are seeking a reprieve from their everyday lives—physical touch, validation, or long-needed orgasmic relief. Many of these men are accustomed to the dance—some even show up with a prepared list of desires.

Others arrive in full defensive mode—shields up, armor on, vulnerability checked—the result of a lifetime of being shamed, denied, and shut down in the face of their desires. Time and again, I witness vulnerability, awkwardness, and the uncomfortable game of keeping up walls while these men determine how safe it might be to ask for what they want.

I don't blame them one bit for their nerves. Just the act of seeking out the services of a sex worker—sending that text or making that call—can be terrifying. There's no guarantee you'll be emotionally received in that situation or even have a good time. It's perfectly logical and natural to bring trepidation, fear, or defensiveness into the room with you. (And of course, the same can be true for any kind of sexual expedition, depending on the context.)

Beneath it all, however, I often sense resilience. After all, those I see have already taken the initiative to make the call, show up, and seek touch. They went out of their way to find a space of intimacy and sexual gratification. However nervous they are when they arrive, they've already pushed through whatever resistance they may have had to initiating the process in the first place.

Of course, there are moments of awkwardness as they gauge their sense of safety and willingness to trust me. Over time, just being naked, along with the blend of touch, passion, and even conversations and storytelling, creates a sort of alchemy. The ease makes its way in. If or when it happens, that palpable fear of rejection melts away—sometimes over the course of a single session, sometimes over a greater span of time. Every experience is different.

As the men I work with feel seen, heard, and accepted for who they are, they become more willing to talk about bigger issues in their lives—challenges with their bodies, struggles with self-esteem, and even past traumas. They speak of their struggles to be seen—or to avoid being seen. I hear raw, heartfelt stories that few others in their lives know about.

These accounts aren't just stories; they're confessions of battles fought in silence. Each story is unique, yet they all echo a common desire for understanding and acceptance. I get to witness and hear about their victories as well.

In my memoir, *Every Grain of Sand*, I wrote about a man named Mark who had just come out of a coma and had a surgery scar that zigzagged across his body. Mark felt alone and hopeless in his despair. After his partner abandoned him in his darkest hour, he wasn't about to trust anyone again. In a last-ditch attempt at hope, he reached out to me. When I met Mark, he was vacant of any self-worth and had all but given up, languishing alone in a tiny apartment with what few belongings he had left. I remember he credited his cat as the only thing keeping him from ending it all.

Mark was terrified of being touched again. Our encounter was complicated but beautiful. He was resistant at first, but once I earned his trust, the relief and realization that things were going to be OK was unmistakable. The floodgates opened, and what happened in that room was a renewal of spirit—pure, erotic, orgasmic letting go.

Our short time together tipped the scales toward possibility for Mark. From his darkest parts, a resilience emerged. By giving space to his struggles—the self-loathing, distrust, resentment, anger, and abandonment—we unwittingly used these uninvited emotions as fuel for our fire.

After our encounter, Mark and I stayed friendly, but I never saw him again professionally. I followed him on social media and watched as he began to come alive again. He took risks and broke down some of his emotional walls. One evening, during his nightly walk around the neighborhood, by random chance, he met the love of his life.

Perhaps it wasn't so random. Perhaps it was because he'd opened up to the possibility of love. From there, things took off. He got married and became involved in his community. I was always so inspired by his story. Once he peeked behind the curtain and glimpsed the possibilities available to him, he began living his life to the fullest. Once he discovered that he was worthy of love and joy, he seemed unstoppable.

It would dishonor his memory not to mention that after a few years of his new life, Mark eventually died of pneumonia. However, he did not die alone, feeling broken and unlovable. He died surrounded by love and by a life lived on purpose.

We don't always get to experience such a lovely story of victory over adversity with such dramatic flair. Not every journey bends so palpably toward sexual freedom, like Mark's did. However, I believe his story illustrates how changing our relationship to our emotions and traumatic experiences can transform us—without needing to exile our difficult feelings. Again, when we allow the room to be more expansive, we are better able to show up for what is present.

THE BURDEN OF SHAME

You may find this hard to believe, but even with my breadth of experience, old insecurities or the occasional awkwardness of sex still visit me. I'll say it again—we don't necessarily shed these issues so much as we learn to allow them space in the room as well.

Sexual shame is what first inspired me to create this work. During my years of sex work, I witnessed the shame men carried—each in his own way, but also in an unmistakably similar way. This is when I knew I had the insights to bring this topic to light.

What happens when we're ashamed of who we are? What happens if we feel, on any level, that our very being is problematic? Or if our queerness—our identity—is a problem to solve? Do we find ourselves at a disadvantage as we navigate the field of sex, love, and intimacy? Does our shame paralyze us or block us from being who we are?

What can we cultivate when we approach these issues with more curiosity and less judgment? What does it feel like to open ourselves up to more possibilities? At one time or another, many of us have felt guilty after sex. Even more perversely, we may experience shame just for wanting sex in the way we want it. Maybe we have a fetish we believe is taboo. Maybe we hold beliefs that tell us sex in general is simply shameful.

Growing up feeling ashamed creates confusion and frustration, which can often manifest as resentment, anger, and hostility. Shame can shut us down and push us into isolation. We become experts at avoiding our feelings, pushing them down or to the side. How often do you lock away emotions you've labeled as "bad"?

Many of us have tried to self-medicate our way out of these feelings. We use alcohol or drugs to create a lubricant for sexual connection. There's an ongoing meth epidemic in the gay community, and evidence shows it's tied to the inability to form genuine connections. Recreational drugs like methamphetamine, GHB, and even ecstasy can create a false sense of connection while lowering inhibitions. But prolonged, compulsive, or addictive use often results in consequences that are difficult to navigate. If you're familiar with the cycle of addiction, you know this hamster wheel only leads to a much harder path. Where there's addiction, there's often shame.

Shame is also closely tied to experiences of bullying and violence. It lies at the root of many cultural issues that are both destructive and disempowering. Bullying behavior often comes from someone deeply afraid of their own sexuality, shaped by their cultural upbringing. And there are certainly people who bully out of hatred and fear of what they don't understand. Time and again, we hear stories of rabidly homophobic individuals being exposed as gay themselves, often public figures in positions of power. Their hypocrisy—born from shame and ignorance—has caused immeasurable harm and further marginalized queer people.

Even today, some countries have laws that condemn queer individuals to lives of unbearable pain and terror. These cultures have horrific consequences for the communities they affect, because shame is fear-based and can provoke visceral, sometimes violent reactions, including mob mentality both online and in local communities.

Overzealous religious ideology plays a huge role in cultural shame. The church, in general, has done very little to mitigate the death spiral they created centuries ago, pitting communities against those who don't conform to their systems of terror and control. The ripple effect of shame seeps into almost every area of our world—it has tentacles in houses of religion, courts of morality, seats of Congress, and lands squarely in the living rooms of every home. Our ability to emerge from such depths as queer people is one of our superpowers.

On a more personal level, as we've explored in the Room of the Thinking Mind, the Room of the Emotions is also a place to cultivate observation and witness our emotions without becoming engulfed by them. For many, achieving this state of observation is no easy feat, especially during charged moments: a scathing remark from someone close, the sting of a relationship's end, echoes of past body shaming, or the loaded risks of a sexual environment.

Left unaddressed, these wounds can fester and evolve into corrosive beliefs about our self-worth, inciting a sense of undesirability. Shame can also be subtle and hard to discern in ourselves when we've carried it so long it has become woven into our lives.

People often give me examples of how shame can be healthy, but I believe this requires a deeper conversation. They often apply the "should feel" idea about shame where guilt is a better descriptor. For this work, I'm apt to speak to the shame we feel from judgment and self-defeating experiences. Assuming most folks reading this book have a moral compass, I doubt we need a refresher on guilt.

THE WEIGHT OF JUDGMENT

Many gay men have experienced incredible amounts of judgment in their lives. As a result, they've become quite skilled at being judgmental—both toward themselves and the world around them.

We might think judgment belongs more in the Room of the Thinking Mind, but it also finds a home in the Room of the Emotions. Shame, isolation, despair, and loneliness often take center stage when judgment arrives. When we feel isolated or a sense of not belonging, it's easy to become judgmental as a defense mechanism, telling ourselves stories about why we feel the way we do. We might blame a group of people for being snobbish or not inclusive. We may decide the city we live in isn't friendly and that it's too difficult to make "real friends." The common thread in all of this is that we tend to look outwardly instead of inwardly for the source of these feelings.

Judgment separates us and is often distorted by the lens through which we view the world. If our wound is touched, if we feel ashamed, or if we operate from a sense of "wrong being," it becomes easier to fall into the paradigm of "this is good," "this is bad," "this is right," "this is wrong." We begin to identify and label our experiences through judgment. This is a great place to use noticing as a tool. We might start an inner conversation with, "I notice that I'm judging. I notice that I have an opinion. I notice a sense of wrongness. I notice I feel ashamed." Or, "I notice I'm feeling guilty."

The act of noticing can help cultivate compassion. Judgment becomes a different animal when we get curious about other possibilities and wonder what else is available. What would happen if you could experience that judgment . . . wait for it . . . nonjudgmentally? Take a moment to notice your thoughts and feelings, or even allow them to come freely. What if you gave the same room, the same grace, to any self-judgments that may arise in this process?

In recovery circles, we often hear, "We meet them where they are," referring to someone with substance use disorders who may be only partly committed to getting clean. It would be unfair if I couldn't do the same for myself—meeting myself where I am today. I say this because sometimes we criticize ourselves, then criticize the critic within us, which just puts us on another hamster wheel.

What happens when we allow ourselves to be who we are, judgments and all? Can we get curious about the idea that there's room for all the voices, including the ones that don't seem, on the surface, to be helpful?

The hope here is that we allow the compassionate voice to move us toward who we want to embody beyond our opinions and judgments, so we can live beyond the shame they bring. Shame no longer gets to fill the entire room, but it can still remain. The less we resist it, the less it dominates the conversation.

What happens when we release the idea that we must conquer or dismiss our feelings or label them as inherently bad? We tend to identify so much with our moods, emotions, and fears that they start to feel like exactly that—a piece of our identity—rather than something we are simply experiencing.

THE WALL OF ANXIETY

As we delve deeper into the Room of the Emotions, let's turn to a conversation I had with a friend while we were sitting at my kitchen table. "I'm just having a really bad day," he confided. "I'm afraid I'm going to lose my job because my anxiety is affecting my performance." His voice, heavy with the weight of his struggles, filled the room. I listened, giving him the space he needed, before gently reminding him, "You have every right to feel the way you do right now."

Let's unpack this. When we fixate on a distressing emotion like anxiety, it can grow in our minds until it feels insurmountable. This feeling—whether it's anxiety, self-doubt, guilt, shame, or any form of self-criticism—can quickly become a relentless cycle of negativity. It's like staring at a blank wall so closely that the rest of the room blurs into insignificance.

I posed a metaphor to my friend. "If your anxiety were a wall blocking your path, imagine only seeing the stark whiteness of that barrier. Now, step back. The room grows. Other walls, the ceiling, and the floor—they all come into perspective. The wall doesn't vanish, but it's no longer your entire view."

I could see this visual struck a chord with him, prompting me to ask, "Are you making room for anxiety or trying to push it away?"

He admitted, somewhat reluctantly, "I wish it would just go away."

Here again lies a common misconception: the relentless quest for a solution. We're programmed to conquer problems. But anxiety isn't a puzzle—it's an experience. It has no interest in your attempts to suppress or change it. It exists as part of the human condition. While it's far more prevalent in some, it exists in all of us. What might happen if we acknowledge anxiety's presence and take interest in its ability to paralyze us? Even more, what if we could remind ourselves—and maybe even live by the idea—that our feelings belong to us, not the other way around?

Additionally, I might try to become aware of my relationship to anxiety. Am I trying to rid myself of it or lock it away? Do I seek out ways to dampen it with alcohol or other substances? Will I dive headlong into some class or course that promises to change how I feel?

Visionaries and spiritual leaders often talk about the equation "pain x resistance = suffering." When our emotions are painful, it's natural to resist experiencing them. But that resistance causes more suffering than necessary. Think about getting an injection in your arm—if you tense up and resist, the injection will hurt more than if you're relaxed. The question isn't how to avoid the sting of that shot—it's about allowing our feelings in a way that mitigates the pain or fear that may hold sway over us.

The thing you fear may happen—rejection, unwanted feelings, misunderstandings. But can you be willing to ease into the impact, observe it, rub the spot where it hurts, and then turn your attention to the wisdom the emotion offers? Our job here is not to endure the pain and surrender our power. It's simply to allow ourselves the space to acknowledge the pain, acknowledge the resistance, and not beat ourselves up about it further.

THE STORIES WE WRITE

In 2010, I was traveling in Hong Kong, and I found myself with a couple of days to kill before my travel companion arrived. I had heard that the highest bungee jump in the world was just a ferry ride away in Macau, the Las Vegas of China. Being the cocksure adventurer I painted myself to be, I decided to do the jump. I went all the way up to the top of the Macau Tower, 1,100 feet high—only 300 feet shy of jumping off the Empire State Building.

When I got to the tiny platform and looked down, I was terrified. I was standing on a platform barely big enough for my feet and the operator's. Everything below me was skyscrapers, hotels, and casinos. Being above them all made for a trembling, destabilizing awareness. I started to shake and immediately began making excuses. My head started writing a story: "The instructor wasn't clear enough. I couldn't understand him because of his accent. This jump is too dangerous." My knees knocked together, and my head swirled, grasping for any reason to dismount that platform. I was convinced I would never jump 1,100 feet. Every fiber of my being knew I could die.

One of the other bungee rig operators, a sarcastic and very confident Australian, saw how panicked I was. He put his hand on my shoulder, looked me in the eyes, and said, "Mate, very few people die doing this, and chances are you won't be one of them." He said it with a smug smile. Then he made me a bet: "If you do this jump, I bet you a beer you'll run back up here begging to do it again." He was hanging onto my harness and asked me to trust him—and for some reason, I did. He released my harness, and down I went.

It was the most mind-blowing free fall I'd ever experienced. Peaceful and easy. My fear and terror were alive and kicking, right alongside this incredible experience. I landed safely, easily, and yes, I ran back up and begged to do it again.

This is similar to how we cultivate our sense of inadequacy. It begins when I think I'm about to do something really cool—like going on that date with Mr. Right Now, planning to have mind-blowing sex at the play party, or heading to the club. I'll be getting dressed, and then—boom! Suddenly, the floodgates of "what ifs" open. Enter, maybe you've heard this phrase before: "the paralysis of analysis." I start in on how fat I look, how the crowd will be too young or too old, how I won't be noticed, or some other story of self-sabotage. What's the fear? What am I afraid of? In many ways, it's the fear of rejection—not being wanted or not getting my desires met. So I craft a story about what could happen or what is happening, to get myself to safety as quickly as possible, avoiding the rejection entirely.

None of this is to convince you that you need to change your story or rewrite it. What I encourage is to allow it to be there. But also, don't ignore the multiple other possibilities happening at the same time. The bungee jump is a great analogy for how we build a narrative that paralyzes us with fear, convincing us that our feelings of not-enoughness are the only story that's true.

Here's what I find so interesting: I've since bungee-jumped many times, all over the planet, and every time, the story is the same. I get onto the platform, and fear and terror arrive. My head tells me it's too dangerous.

My fear tries to consume my actions or inactions, convincing me I can't do this today. The brain looks for a way out, to survive. And it's almost like a brand-new experience every time, as if I've never felt this fear before—even though I have, many times. It doesn't go away. What changes is my relationship with fear. It doesn't get to take center stage, even though the story still shows up—or at least tries to.

What I've learned is that I don't get to bungee-jump my way out of fear. I am afraid, and at the same time, I know there's another story jumping with me. I am safe, I am capable, and I can enjoy the fall, the excitement, and the adrenaline. Had I backed out of that jump, I would've been the one telling myself how unworthy I was, or rationalizing how dangerous it had been and how I'd dodged a bullet. We write the story however we see fit to keep ourselves safe.

Likewise, in the moments before having sex, or when you're about to engage with someone you're attracted to, we get nervous. We all do. The story begins: maybe it's "There's no way they're into me," or "I'm too fat," or "I'm ugly." These thoughts often cultivate feelings of fear, inadequacy, dread, or shame. And as we've discussed in the previous sections, these messages come from everywhere. Instead of trying to eliminate thoughts of unworthiness, nervousness, or fear of rejection—or whatever critique you have of yourself—notice it. Notice the story you write about it. Notice how you're experiencing it, whether it's welcomed or rejected. Are you exiling this feeling, this story, to a room with a locked door, put away and isolated?

What I'm asking is: when a sense of inadequacy, fear of rejection, dread, or shame arises and begins to take over, do you spin those feelings into a narrative that defines your identity? The sense of dread or fear of rejection is real—it's the observable emotional experience. But the story we often write about ourselves based on these experiences is usually steeped in our own not-enoughness. Is it possible that, somewhere in there, you've come to embody your unworthiness? You come to live it, and be it. "Hello, my name is Unworthy."

And when I say "you," I mean the hundreds of men I've known who have told me their version of this same story. It's a profoundly shared experience, in a million different ways. Some of us are far more hypnotized by what's wrong with us than by what's right, or what else is true. What would it be like to allow this story to be there and get curious? By asking, "What else—and who else—is possible here?" This inner conversation allows us to shift the language without pushing away the observable experience. We can create a more empowering narrative and move away from the expectation that we'll rid ourselves of these feelings.

I'm not saying the story we write is always untrue. But I am saying it's worth noticing the difference in how we speak it, the kind of inner dialogue that shows up. This can be subtle, driven by semantics, but when put into practice, it can be powerfully meaningful. For example: "I am too old and ugly; nobody wants to fuck me," versus "Right now, I'm feeling afraid that I'm too old and ugly, and nobody will want to fuck me." Or even better: "Right now, I'm feeling insecure about my body and my age, and I also know for a fact that I'm incredibly generous, lovely, kind, and a great lover."

What version, or versions, of you are showing up during these moments of paralyzing emotions? Can you ask yourself, as we discussed earlier, "Who else is possible here?" This is also a great time to revisit what is working, what fits, and what brings ease and self-acceptance. When we take stock of what else is true about us—beyond the imprints, the self-talk, and the not-enoughness—what if you didn't need to feel any different about your perceived unworthiness at all to move forward? What if you could let those stories sit alongside other validating stories and truths that you get to uncover—stories that may have been put away or left undiscovered?

Making the room bigger requires more space and ideas about who you are, and who else is hiding behind the curtain of doubt, fear, and old messages you've carried because they kept you safe.

To be clear, none of what I'm talking about—literally none of it—is about making fear disappear. There's no quick fix for that.

IDENTIFYING WITH OUR FEELINGS

When we say things like "I am angry" or "I am lonely," it's easy for those emotions to infiltrate our sense of self. We become the anger, the loneliness, or the not-enoughness, forgetting who we truly are. As I see it, rather than becoming these feelings, we're experiencing them.

Consider the shift that happens when we change our dialogue from "I am angry" to "I feel angry." On one hand, it might seem like semantics since both statements mean roughly the same thing. But the difference is profound—it's the difference between "being" our feelings and "being with" our feelings.

Most of us grew up hearing and using the language of "being" our feelings. But we can practice a new way of speaking. We can shift our relationship to our perceived inadequacies and the imprints that still poke us from time to time, without letting them dominate. Does the language we use to talk to ourselves keep fueling feelings of undesirability? The more we perceive ourselves as unattractive, the more we shrink. The more we shrink, the more we become invisible, and our emotions begin to dominate our identity. Then, boom! We're trapped in the same vicious cycle again, projecting that supposed identity to the world.

Let's practice this idea. How does it feel to say, "Nobody will want to date someone like me. I'm lonely, and I'm too afraid of rejection. I mean, just look at me—I'm a mess!"

Now, what if the inner conversation went more like this: "I notice I feel afraid and lonely right now. I notice I'm fearful of not being liked or desirable. I notice I'm experiencing anxiety." What's it like to bring awareness to what you're noticing?

Let's say you're at a bar, a party, or any setting where sex is happening or expected. You feel exposed—the excitement, anxiety, and insecurity rise inside you. This mix of feelings sets off your hyperarousal or acute stress response. You're probably familiar with the fight-flight-freeze-fawn response. Typically, when we're in danger, our bodies and instincts engage in survival mode. But why does this happen when it's supposed to be a fun, erotic, and sexually engaging time?

We don't have to look much further than our list of people and experiences that lead us to believe our desires are wrong. But there's no need to rehash the sources of our imprints—the point is asking ourselves how we can walk through these responses without allowing them to consume us.

This response isn't new. Many gay men know it all too well—that particular mix of nerves that buzz just before stepping into a sexually charged environment. Our emotions often drive our actions, and when fear and insecurity take over, we risk missing out on fulfilling sexual encounters and meaningful connections. But that's only if fear and insecurity are the only emotions we make room for.

What if, instead of dismissing nervousness or fear of rejection, we acknowledge them? Give them a nod, and begin the inner inquiry by noticing. Have that internal conversation with yourself. Pause and check in with your feelings, instead of jumping straight into action or reaction. Ask yourself, "What am I noticing right now?"

Maybe place your hand on your abdomen and say, "I notice I'm nervous right now." Pause and breathe. "I notice I'm fearing rejection." Pause and breathe. "I notice a sense of anxiety." It's perfectly OK to say, "I don't know what the fuck I'm noticing, but I'm feeling something uncomfortable!" Take a long pause, a deep breath. Then, move into the questions: "What else is possible here? What does it feel like to be unafraid? Who else is possible here? What would it be like to go for it?"

Nervousness is often just one element in a more complex mix of emotions we experience in our quest for a sexually enriching experience. Combine that with judgment, insecurities, and illusions of inadequacy, and sometimes sexually charged expectations can be overwhelming. And if that's the case, so be it! There's no need to force it.

I readily admit, I've been at sex parties, ready to cross the threshold, only to grab my stuff and go home to eat ice cream. And yes, I judged myself for not following through. I told myself, "You chickened out," but

I also reminded myself, "You're taking care of yourself. You're loving yourself. You're protecting yourself." My point is that our emotions are powerful, so I encourage you to be gentle with yourself. And of course, eat lots of ice cream. The courage will return, and desire will always be there, so give yourself plenty of grace.

Can we be with fear and loneliness while also naming what we desire? "I'm in fear, and I want to connect with someone, be touched, fucked, kissed deeply. I want to feel sexy, and I'm also experiencing anxiety around that. I notice I'm fearful of rejection." Don't forget to ask: Who else is possible here? What else might be possible that I'm not seeing right now?

You can have an inner conversation and call forward your own curiosity. Being in tune with your feelings creates space. Expanding the Room of the Emotions gives you time to refine the language of your self-talk.

What gets created if we don't make space? If I judge an emotion, I might exile the idea of feeling afraid, insecure, or unacceptable, rather than allowing, observing, noticing, and getting curious about that feeling. Once I decide that I'm unacceptable or afraid, and that the emotion is "bad," the practice of avoiding it, pushing it down, or drowning it out becomes not just an attempt to solve the problem but also the solution. *If I'm bad and don't belong, then I won't go—and I'll stay safe.*

It helps to practice being a witness to your full experience and allowing possibilities to arrive. We can cultivate curiosity. We might find that it takes less energy to do so than to constantly separate the good from the bad, the wanted feelings from the unwanted, or the sense of unworthiness from the sense of worthiness.

The feelings you perceive as undesirable have no more power than you give them. Let me be clear: I'm not suggesting that our thoughts, beliefs, emotions, imprints, and personal histories don't weigh heavily on us. But I'm asking you to consider whether resisting them is actually saving you any effort or sparing you any unhappiness.

WHAT HAPPENS WHEN I FEEL?

People in our lives often ask us, "How do you feel?" What if we put a twist on that familiar phrase and asked ourselves, "What happens when I feel?"

Consider that question not as an inquiry about your current state of mind but as one aimed at how you respond to various emotions. This response can be tangible, like shaking hands, a fast-beating heart, or a need to escape. It can also manifest on an intangible level, such as a sense of not belonging or the belief that the emotion makes you weak.

With this in mind: How do you respond when you get angry? How do you feel anger?

What happens when shame creeps in? How do you feel shame?

What do you do with your emotions? Think about the last time you felt anxiety, unworthiness, joy, or anger. Reflect on your actions, thoughts, internal responses, and any subsequent feelings when this emotion hits you. The goal is to become aware of how we react within our emotional space.

This is a great time to grab a journal or notepad. Make a list of emotions you struggle with or that are prevalent in your life and write a few down. For example: The last time I was lonely, I started to doom-scroll on social media. The last time I got angry, I shut down and isolated myself.

Reflect on what kind of outward behavior comes forward. Examples include: When I feel joyful, I tend to get hyper and act extroverted. When I feel insecure, I tend to isolate or avoid overwhelming situations.

Remember the event, then allow the feelings if you can. Take note of what happens when you feel sadness, excitement, or any other emotion. Try not to overthink this. Don't look for conclusions or for any particular change to take root. The process is like planting a seed to see what gets created, but let that happen (or not happen) in its own time.

Next, explore the ways you manage emotions when you're uncomfortable. Do you opt for a glass of wine or alcohol, drugs, exercise, meditation, supportive conversation, sex, self-pleasure, or something else? What about a prevalent sexual memory? What was the physical sensation that accompanied that feeling? What kind of emotions arose?

Does that information offer you anything new? Is it possible to simply observe the memory without feeling triggered in any way? (It's OK if the answer is no.) How are you trying to resist or avoid feelings?

Avoidance is a response to many uncomfortable emotions. I become distractible when I feel something uncomfortable. I may isolate or become paralyzed, unable to make a decision or take action toward my desires when I avoid experiencing my emotions. The wound can be so tender and painful that I want to avoid touching it at all costs. But what does it really cost me to avoid touching the wound?

At first, isolation may feel safe, warm, and comforting, but after a while, it can turn into loneliness. Then, being left alone with ongoing ideas of not-enoughness or unworthiness shows up. I sit in the shadows, not daring to take a chance on hooking up, going out, or trying to connect because my feelings are teaming up with my false beliefs and assumptions about what might happen. It's a recipe for overwhelming self-loathing, and it can shut us down.

Sometimes the wound feels unbearable, too tender to explore, and the pain is so intense that I'm almost forced to do something about it. Seeking help—picking up the 500-pound phone, sending that text message to a trusted friend or a professional—is hard.

There's a common refrain among those of us in recovery called "doing it by the pain method." We swim around in our wounds and remain in isolation because it feels familiar. It might even feel easier. The wound is still there because our emotions—tied to our beliefs about unworthiness—are still running the show. Only when we are in enough pain will we reach out for help or seek something that offers relief. For addicts and people who experience substance dependency, it's often excessive alcohol or drug use to blot out or dull the pain, even if only temporarily.

A great deal of the men I've worked with don't want to experience rejection, so they don't go into that bar, don't cruise that app, don't approach that guy, and won't have that discussion with their partner. Even more isolating is the stigma of loneliness that this creates, which prevents most men from talking about it with their friends. It's easier to just jack off in the shower, avoiding intimacy—but at what cost?

When it comes to sex, love, and intimacy, the fact is, life shows up, and at some point, we may get an opportunity to put ourselves out there. What happens when we make the room big enough to allow both our fear of rejection and our desire to engage to be in the room at the same time?

As we move on from the Room of the Emotions, I encourage us to keep asking ourselves whether managing our feelings serves us, and if so, how. Is avoiding them a release valve or a wall we've built? What would it be like to make the room bigger so we can fully experience our feelings? Remember, all of our feelings are important, valued, and sacred.

TAKE A WELLNESS WALK

I invite you to embody this practice by going for a nice, long walk. Allow yourself to experience the full range of emotions. Pay attention to the stories you're telling yourself, welcoming any and all ideas into the room.

You will need to grab your music device and earbuds for this and create a playlist to set the tone. Look for songs that evoke a particular response in you. There might be a song that always reminds you of a certain break-up, how much you love a certain person in your life, or even awkward memories from high school dances. Fill your playlist with songs that are sad, empowering, upbeat, slow, or moody. Include anthems, dance music—anything that moves you. It doesn't matter what mood or feeling you're going for, as long as it's not merely background music. The point of this exercise is to experience your feelings. Notice them. Allow them. Observe them.

You might recall an uncomfortable memory of a moment you shared with someone. You may experience regret, remorse, or a sense of loss. Or you might feel joy, victory, happiness—whatever it is, be with the experience. Think about "feeling" as a verb, not a noun. It's something we do. We feel things. So, what are you feeling?

Now, pay attention to where your mind wanders. For the purposes of this work, practice paying attention and becoming a witness. Where do you feel that emotion? Does it create a tightness in your throat? A ball of energy in your solar plexus? Wherever it registers, allow it. Don't let yourself go down a path that's too difficult to navigate and lose the point. For this exercise, make sure you control the experiment.

Orchestrate your emotions and practice becoming aware of what gets created in the experience. This exercise is about bringing awareness to what happens when we intentionally feel our emotions. Have fun with it. I absolutely encourage you to journal and practice being with your feelings.

SEXUAL AWARENESS IN *QUEER*Y

Let's revisit this exercise to explore what's happening in the Room of the Emotions. Remember, there are no right or wrong answers—simply consider these questions and see what comes up. If you like, use a journal to note any feelings that arise.

Reflect on the last time you had an orgasm or engaged in sexual pleasure. This could include self-pleasure, a hookup, cruising on the street, a scheduled sex-work appointment (massage, escort, live cam show, etc.), online sexting, sex with a partner, etc.

What stands out about this experience? Were you fantasizing, checking out, being in the moment, engaging in critical self-talk, or considering it an act of self-care? How were you feeling? Were you frustrated, nervous, or excited? It's OK if you can't remember the details.

Do you have a favorite way to get off, such as watching porn, fantasizing, using toys, getting blow jobs, jacking off, or getting penetrated? Do you notice any feelings or judgments about your preferences?

Throughout your day and the week ahead, remember to practice asking empowering questions—and to live in those questions rather than try to answer them. Allow ideas and answers to arrive on their own. Your role is simply to observe and gather insights you can use.

THE SACRED

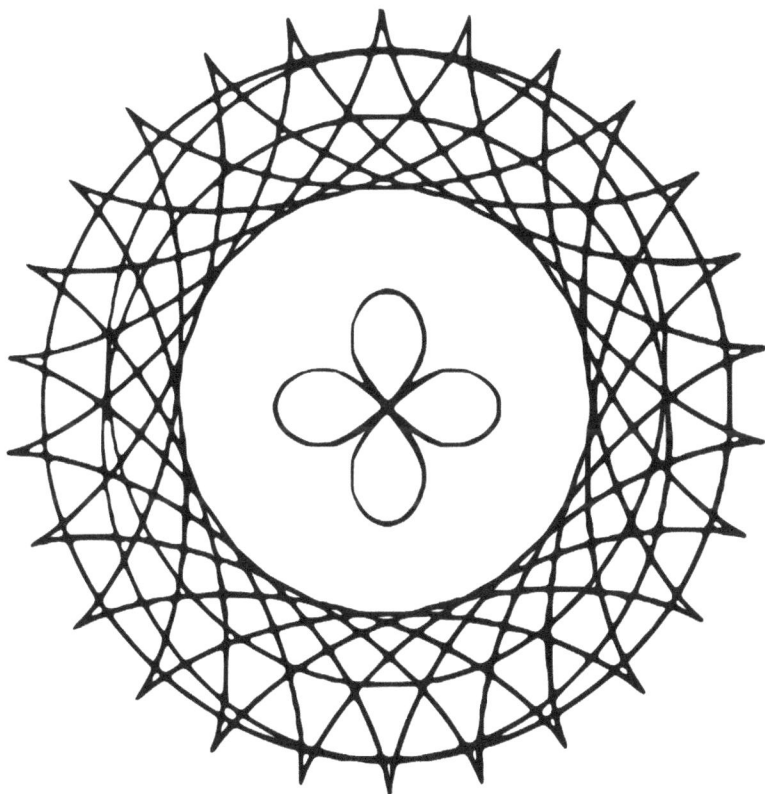

III

THE ROOM OF THE SACRED

I've really been looking forward to this section because it's the foundation of the work I do in the world. I believe sex is sacred, and it's essential for our health.

If I can take a moment for a bit of a rant here: I've heard the call of many well-meaning sacred intimates and sex coaches who claim that sex and intimacy are very different things, and that having one without the other is "not in alignment and causes dis-ease in your sacral chakra," or that it's the reason for your unhappiness and loneliness. I've read countless comments and blogs that say, "hookup culture has robbed queer men of the spiritual nature of sex." I've watched video after video of practitioners selling retreats and healing sessions, promising to restore your authentic sexual spirit.

I don't argue with their reality. It's easy to find evidence that this phenomenon might hold some truth. After all, we live in a world where many believe they are broken and in need of something special to make their wholeness stick. And don't get me wrong—there are many providers who are genuinely in the business of uncovering the best in people, and I love these men dearly. But I get a little befuddled when I hear declarations like, "hookup culture is so bad for you," or "sex for the fun of sex removes its magic." *Insert David's litany of curse words here.*

I guess what I'm trying to say is that sex is very much a part of the human condition. It's an absolute part of our well-being, and it's sacred—even just regular fun sex.

I have yet to meet a person who says, "I want meaningless, disjointed, and empty experiences with others." What I do hear men say is that they want connected sexual experiences, and I always ask them how that looks, what that means—and very few can put it into words. What I've discovered is that meaningful connections look different to different people and shift from moment to moment, day to day. Sometimes it means just showing up as who we are right now. If we consider all the variables, we could honestly say that sometimes it's a cock in your mouth, and other times it's an intimate connection—with various versions of this along a spectrum.

Most of the men I've worked with are, in fact, seeking the sacred. So, what do I mean by sacred if there isn't some hierarchy that places sacredness above recreational sex, which some would unfortunately call "low-vibration" behavior? My biggest gripe with the low-vibe/high-vibe sex analogy is that it risks pathologizing sex, leading to terms like "sex addiction" and "compulsive sexual behavior" being thrown around. Entire wellness programs are built around these ideas and further cultivate opportunities to deepen shame.

I'm not here to argue the merits of different modalities of care in sexual medicine, but I do caution us, as queer men, to consider how easily we lean into the disease model paradigm. Society has already done a great job of that to us for eons.

WHAT IS SACRED?

The word *sacred* can be so loaded for some people—particularly those who come from religious backgrounds—that I almost didn't use it here.

Sacred doesn't mean something is better. It simply means it's revered and beautiful—it's something we cherish with intense love and compassion. If the religious association is an obstacle for you, I encourage you to think of this as the Room of Values and Desires. What's sacred is what you find most meaningful, whether it's tangible, such as your sex life, or intangible, such as your personal values. You might say I'm reclaiming the word *sacred* from the exclusively religious connotations that my personal history and imprints once layered on it—much like how we've reclaimed the word *queer* from its history as a weapon used against us.

This section isn't about some mysterious, omnipresent energy with unexplainable powers that invisibly connects humanity and makes us all one. That's not to say there isn't space for that if you want it. Sometimes the universe speaks to you, and the ability to listen can be important—especially in terms of living in the questions and practicing the art of allowing.

If we explore our ideas of what's sacred with the mindset of an archaeologist—seeking out treasures and artifacts from the rubble of our imprints and wounds—we can begin to understand what's blocking our entry to the Room. We can fill the Room with what we want most in our lives and sift through the dusty old artifacts that no longer hold sway over us, setting them aside. It may have been a long time since we truly connected with what's meaningful to us, as we've often been buried beneath our longing for connection and self-acceptance.

Many of us see safety and trust as sacred. Community, for many, is also sacred. What about the freedom to covet nudity? Maybe you objectify a specific body type, worship the phallus, or enjoy a form of sexual kink. Maybe it's a type of porn you use for self-pleasure. There are countless treasures yet to be discovered.

My point is that what belongs in the Room of the Sacred is you—your idea of what's meaningful, what you're passionate about, what you love, and what you want to cultivate in your life. There are no right or wrong, good or bad ideas in this room. If your way of experiencing what you hold sacred or meaningful in the world of sex, love, and intimacy is raunchy or salacious, or if it has an air of mystery, or even if sitting at home cooking a meal is meaningful to you—so be it. In this room, we get to define what's sacred to each of us. We get to have a deeply personal experience with what matters. In the Room of the Sacred, we prioritize what we want as we uncover it.

It can be difficult to name what's sacred if we're steeped in shame and a sense of not belonging. The same goes if we've spent large portions of our lives—or are currently experiencing—a sense of emptiness or loneliness. Shame and low self-worth have tentacles that stretch through so many areas of our existence that it can seem bleak to conjure ideas of what's meaningful and sacred. Our desires—especially when our culture or imprints tell us they're something to be ashamed of—can bring up doubts, fears, and a sense of unworthiness. In turn, this shame crowds out any notion of what we might hold as sacred. Our sense of wrongness or the judgment of others causes our self-worth to plummet. Once we've created a world for ourselves that is "unholy" and not sacred, we play small.

Early childhood memories of being cast out, branded a sinner, or deemed unacceptable block us from identifying what we consider sacred. We may change who we are to fit into other people's ideas of what's acceptable. We might try to manage situations and others' reactions by people-pleasing. Or we might isolate ourselves, drink to oblivion, or work too hard. Identifying these strategies requires deep inquiry—and finding our way out can be an adventure, to say the least. It's easy to render our sexual spaces unworthy of sacredness and meaning. The journey into this room requires climbing through the rocks and sifting through these ruins to a space where we can define what we deem sacred and desirable.

We begin by asking: What do you truly care about? What brings meaningfulness to the room? Many of us long for connection and to feel desirable. We all want to feel safe and comfortable in our own skin. Are there places that are sacred to you? Where do you find sexual freedom? For some, it's a sex club or a bathhouse. For others, it's the cuddle puddle at a men's retreat. Another person's sacred space could be their bedroom, where they enjoy an evening alone with music, a favorite porn movie, and a bottle of lube. What do we value when it comes to finding our pleasure and being turned on?

Many of our most guarded desires are not particularly taboo. Rather, they simply feel wrong on a personal level, such as fantasizing about sex outside of a primary relationship or being dominated. Maybe you have an adventurous fetish, such as being humiliated, or a dirty sex fetish at which even our vibrant LGBTQIA+2 culture turns their nose up. Does that make your desires unholy or not meaningful? Do you conceal them—even the basic desire for sex—or approach them hesitantly?

In the Room of the Sacred, I invite you to gradually expand your perspective. Notice any illusion of unholiness alongside the desire to feel safe so you can explore the deeper, darker edges of our temples. At some point, we will seek what we want. Recognizing the importance of our desires can greatly empower us on the road toward sexual well-being.

Getting there may seem like a winding road from the look of the next chapters but stick with me as we cultivate and take some mental notes on the sacred.

YOUR SACRED HERITAGE

A vital part of finding meaning on our expedition into the Room of the Sacred is to uncover our origins. Where do you come from? Whose shoulders do you stand on? Start tracing your sacred heritage through your location, culture, and country of origin. Then add family members, friends, romantic partners, mentors, and colleagues or other professionals.

It goes without saying that many queer individuals carry deeply painful imprints about their place in the world. For many, even a fleeting moment of being one's true self in some places still represents a considerable risk. While I've urged us to refrain from pointing fingers, we recognize that religious and cultural beliefs have long placed queer individuals in the line of fire. That said, I also want to carve out a space to celebrate who you are and the origins you hail from.

There's something affirming about hearing tales of my ancestors. I've always been eager to discover who these long-departed relatives were and how I might connect with their legacies. The stories I did hear, though few, were thrilling and occasionally melancholic, but I cherished whatever knowledge I could glean. I was especially thrilled to learn that I have a trans nephew, the only other queer person in my family (that I know of) besides myself. Perhaps I was searching for glimpses of myself in those stories or seeking a sense of belonging. It felt safer to be part of an ancestral lineage—dead people can't judge you—than to be labeled undesirable within my own family and community.

There are certain perks to being part of queer culture. We are, collectively, well-practiced at creating our chosen families. We're historically ahead of the curve as norm-breakers, peacemakers, and sexual freedom fighters, as well as artists and creatives. As a queer person, you come from a long lineage of queer, creative, and powerful people: Michelangelo, Leonardo da Vinci, Alan Turing, Elton John, James Baldwin, Alvin Ailey, Lorraine Hansberry, Sally Ride, Billie Jean King, and the list goes on.

These may seem like mighty big shoes to fill, but no one expects you to make the next big discovery or achieve some great accomplishment for humanity. We can simply be proud and unashamed by virtue of knowing where we came from. Whether or not you identify with this rich heritage, the fact is, it belongs to you.

Queer people have been venerated by many cultures for thousands of years. Numerous indigenous cultures recognize the sacredness of LGBTQIA+2 identities. For example, many North American indigenous peoples honor Two-Spirit individuals, who embody both masculine and feminine qualities.

This message resonated deeply with me during my visits to the BAAITS (Bay Area American Indian Two-Spirits) powwow in San Francisco, where I witnessed the honoring of these sacred people and their traditions. Passed down through generations, these traditions continue to be renewed and reclaimed by both the young and the elders, with a dignity that has nearly been erased due to the historical marginalization of First Nations people.

The Navajo, also known as Diné, recognized the "Nádleehi," the Zuni people honored the "lhamana," and in precolonial Africa, the "Isangoma" were revered. In South Asia, the Hijra community holds a similar significance. Historically, in nearly every ancient culture, these individuals played important roles in religious ceremonies and societal events. It is striking that only after the spread of religious indoctrination and colonization did shame befall these once vital and respected members of society.

During the Roman Empire, among the powerful ruling class, same-sex mentoring and bonding were common. Historians have well documented the love and public adoration Emperor Hadrian lavished upon his lover, Antinous, by building temples and statues in his honor.

We've already discussed how queer, bi, trans, and gay men have inherited a lineage of shame, despair, death, and disease. We tend to focus so much on our obstacles that we don't take in other perspectives and see what else may be available. Likewise, it's easy to fixate on the so-called "pain narrative" of being queer—just look at the storytelling in media and entertainment, which is so often centered on these difficult experiences. The result is that we lose track of, or never take stock of, what else is there.

The fact is, we stand on the shoulders of giants.

What is your queer heritage? Who and what has made you who you are? How has your sexuality been supported? Think about cultural influences—historical and current icons in your life, famous or not. Queer people who inspired or influenced you in some way. This includes allies. After all, every gay boy has followed and obsessed over an iconic female superstar, many of whom have befriended our community. The people who have been our North Stars include Judy Garland, Lady Gaga, Liza Minnelli, Stevie Nicks, Cher, Madonna, Kylie Minogue, and so many more. Yes, indeed, our icons are sacred!

There are many paths to uncovering the places and spaces where we feel among our people. I sincerely believe community is sacred—and sometimes crucial. Our sense of belonging is sacred, and we often find that where we have common ground. It's one of the many reasons Pride celebrations exist. It's not just a party or a protest—these events are beacons for the queer person in the Deep South to know there are people out there like them, and that they belong.

Whatever your queer heritage is or whoever has supported you along the way, finding your enough-ness could be instrumental in cultivating a sense of belonging. If you're struggling to discover where you fit in, consider exploring clubs, groups, and places that resonate with who you want to be in the world. How might that serve your whole being? Could engaging with esteemable ideas—like volunteering or community service—help us reclaim our self-esteem? As we unearth our treasures, gently brushing away the soil that blocks our view, we make the room big enough for the people who inspire us.

CREATING CONNECTIONS

Let's talk a little about creating those connections we've long been told are necessary for a fulfilling love life and beyond. There's a really powerful but scary exercise I do from time to time, and believe it or not, it's not as easy as it sounds.

Expressing our gratitude, admiration, and appreciation to those we care about—something we might take for granted or think is simple—can surprise you with how rare and difficult it actually is. Have you ever been to a wedding where the best man makes a deep, meaningful toast that gets everyone in the room emotional? Think of this as a mini or macro version of that. You don't have to wait for a special occasion to practice creating these connections.

Imagine sitting down with someone you truly care about—someone who has supported you in your life, maybe a parent, sibling, or best friend—and expressing to them all the ways in which you're grateful for them. When you do this as a formal, intentional experience, really speaking from the depths of your heart about how they've impacted your life, and setting aside any grievances, it allows you to see and be with them exactly as they are. Being able to share what they mean to you is a beautiful expression of love.

It seems easy, but it can be surprisingly difficult to put into action. Find someone you deeply care about, arrange a dedicated time to be with them, and use that time to convey how significant they are in your life. Tell them you love them. It could be a friend who has been there for you in the past, or even a casual acquaintance. Say something like: "Have I ever really told you how much your friendship means to me?" Or, "I remember when I was out of work, and you called just to check on me. That meant the world to me. Thank you. I love you."

The point is to practice expressing yourself from your heart. Do it via Zoom, or phone if you prefer, or put it in writing. The act of intentional expression, in whatever form, is the point.

Be intentional.

Be kind.

Relinquish expectations.

Cultivating this sense of safety and belonging gives us a boost in self-esteem. When we freely express our gratitude for those who support us, we gain so much from it. Like yoga, don't overstretch yourself—work from where you are now, but do push yourself a little past the point of resistance. The key to this exercise is to express yourself genuinely and honestly, even if it means stepping outside your comfort zone (though that's always optional). You might even want to tell the person you're feeling a little nervous beforehand. In any case, go at your own pace.

Also, keep others in mind as you do this. You're reading a book that focuses on self-activation and taking action, but if your request comes out of nowhere, you might not get the response you're hoping for. You can use this book as a lead-in, introducing the subject by saying something like, "I'm reading this book, and it asks us to do this. I'd love to try it with you."

If it's a quick exchange, let it be what it is. If it turns into a more in-depth conversation, spend that time telling the person what it truly means to have them in your life.

A friend once gave me some great advice: don't sit on compliments. Compliments can be oddly difficult to give sometimes—they bring up insecurities, both about ourselves and about how the other person might react. But here are two things to keep in mind—things that are obvious but which we tend to forget. First, people love to receive compliments. It's a much lower-risk activity than it might seem. And second, even if your expression of appreciation falls flat—if they get uncomfortable, or you get uncomfortable, or both—it's worth the risk. The point is about giving, not about the outcome or fulfilling a set of expectations about what it will do for us.

And remember, you never know when your words might touch someone in a way they'll always appreciate or remember. Instant feedback isn't always guaranteed, but that doesn't mean nothing happened. Again, this isn't something you do for the response you get.

Understanding the unique nature of this exercise might feel weird—good! Be weird!

To challenge yourself further, once you get the hang of it, you might consider trying this exercise with someone you share an intimate or sexual relationship with. What would it be like to say all the things you love about their body, their heart? What if you told them how beautiful they are while lying naked in bed or even during sex? Verbalizing this can be powerful, depending on how receptive they are to hearing it. It might be worth the risk to try it, but remember to read the room. If they express gratitude in return, great! In any case, try not to interrupt the connection. Don't joke or use disclaimers—just be real. Let it play out and see what happens.

Ultimately, this is about making meaningful connections and expressing that to another person. And, just as critically, it's about getting in touch with what this act does to you—your whole being. That's what I try to create in my work and in my everyday life. Ide-ally, I'd like for this kind of emotional generosity to become the norm. To normalize expressing love. Even if it feels weird.

THE GIFTS OF THE SHADOW

In *The Laramie Project*, a play about Matthew Sheph-ard's murder, one of the characters, a priest, refers to Shephard's killers as "our greatest teachers." The idea is alarming out of context. But the priest meant that if we are to understand why someone would commit such a brutal murder out of homophobic hate, we need to consider the perpetrators' unique perspective. They hold information and insight that no one else can give us, if we're serious about understanding and prevent-ing these crimes.

This sentiment applies to how we can learn from our shadows—the recesses of our being where we hide and repress our imprints, wounds, fears, and anything else that dims the light and wisdom we carry within. Our shadows carry information. The shadow and the light are wiser in partnership than either can be alone.

In her classic book, *A Return to Love*, Marianne Wil-liamson writes, "Our deepest fear is not that we are inadequate. Our deepest fear is that we are powerful beyond measure. It is our light, not our darkness, that most frightens us. We ask ourselves, 'Who am I to be brilliant, gorgeous, talented, fabulous?' Actually, who are you not to be? Your playing small does not serve the world. There is nothing enlightened about shrinking so that other people won't feel insecure around you."

That quote captures what I'm getting at here. What if it's not my shadow I fear but my light? What if our imprints and BS beliefs were invitations to find this light? What if your sense that you aren't enough comes from the same part of you that knows you *are* enough? What if underneath the wounds and false beliefs is a whole and worthy being who's been exiled and locked away because we're so invested in our imprints? What if we found out that who we are scares us not because we're inadequate but because we're powerful, loving, and not broken?

Similar to what the priest said about Shepard's killers, I have often thought of my abusers as one of my greatest teachers. They showed me who I am not and who I would never want to be. Likewise, the ways in which we tell ourselves we aren't enough—those messages also carry information and have something to teach us.

The pop culture analogy that comes to mind here is the movie *Close Encounters of the Third Kind*. Though released decades ago, the film was groundbreaking at the time in the way it established "scary aliens" as something other than aggressive monsters. The revelation was that these beings were curious about us—friendly, inquisitive, and collaborative. The breakthrough came when humans traded fear for curiosity and inquiry. Often, the same thing happens in our lives. Our greatest fear turns out to be an ally, an entity with something to offer us. The bridge from living in fear to benefiting from that fear is curiosity and inquiry, maybe even collaboration.

Earlier, we talked about our brilliant strategies—how feeling broken and unloved can be a shield that fortifies our walls. But what are we protecting? Is it our wound or something much more precious? Consider Wayne, the retreat participant I mentioned in the

Room of the Thinking Mind. He'd grown so attached to his imprint—"I'll never find anyone"—that even though he knew it was bullshit, he allowed it to influence his outlook and choices, treating it as a fact rather than a belief.

These are the complexities of the human condition. There may be evidence on the table that we know is bullshit. Yet we'll still use it in the figurative court of opinion against ourselves. The question is, why? What motivates us to hold ourselves back? My instinct tells me Wayne wasn't protecting his shadow—his fear and unworthiness—but rather clinging to that shadow to protect his light from coming into view. In other words, he was keeping his light hidden to protect himself.

Why do we do this? Why prioritize the darkness? Why was it easier for Wayne to buy into his inescapable anxiety than his fondest hope? My instinct tells me that somewhere along the line, likely in early childhood, Wayne decided to protect the lovable, cherishable part of him from the world because others couldn't be trusted with something so important.

We've all been hurt. We've all seen how people can't be trusted, and some of us have experienced that hurt over and over again. All that exposure has stripped us of the ability to open our hearts in ways that feel safe. We might come to believe, "How can I even think about sex when everything is so fucked up?"

Many might call this the innocent inner child—the one who didn't know any better but to love, the one who was inherently lovable—is an essential part of ourselves. It's the default setting—the state of being we're born into—and it's ours to lose to varying degrees along the way. We can think of this part of ourselves as what lies beneath the wound. The aha moment I had with

Wayne—which inspired the sections on imprinting—was that his thinking mind was protecting something precious within him. Something beneath his wound, in the deepest, most vulnerable part of himself. Imagine what you would do to protect your child? Quite a bit, I would imagine.

Early in life, we build a fortress around ourselves out of fear that we might be harmed again. Born from an intense desire to protect the essential love we know we are, we gather resources, access strategies, and buy into bullshit because it keeps us separate and protects the tender part of us we cherish. Over time, as we grow into adolescence and adulthood, we forget why we built the fortress in the first place, so we lose touch with our most essential self—our innocence. We acclimate to this smaller version of ourselves almost without effort.

Much has been written about childhood trauma and the separation from our essence—the part of us that was carefree, curious, living in awe and free self-expression. We have to search for that part of us again. Like an archaeologist in the ruins, our task is to gently brush away the soil to uncover the treasures. We enter ancient tombs and temples, studying our old stories to find the sacred parts of ourselves we've exiled. What we gather leads us to the next adventure—a sexually freer and more dynamic experience of possibility. We can then say with certainty that even our wounds are sacred and meaningful, becoming an ongoing well of wisdom from which we can freely drink.

OUR INNER SWAGGER

What if within us all, there's an energy that moves through the world with a rhythm that feels beautiful and enriching? An energy that makes us attractive in ways we never thought possible.

As we expand the Room of the Sacred, we leave space for a part of ourselves that enhances our confidence, body language, sexual presence, and self-expression—the aspect of our personalities that others see and that defines our interactions with them. Is there a confidence or a knowingness that allows us to be more in tune with our self-worth and to display it for all to see?

Some often mistake this confidence, this inner swagger, as ego and resist expressing the extraordinary or unique part of us that feels sexy and alive. The ego is often narrowly defined as a source of narcissism and dysfunction—something that draws attention out of insecurity and neediness. From this perspective, the ego isn't authentic—it's a mask born of insecurity, a feigned bravado that magnifies our sense of self-importance.

But that's not what I'm talking about here. I'm talking about our *inner swagger*. This part of us is resilient, generous, and lacks nothing. It vibrates love—not just for ourselves but also in service of others. It's a frequency that extends outward and announces, "Here I am!" when we enter the room.

Recently, I was at a men's sex party open to the public. I was outside on the patio, relaxing and enjoying the fall night air. A man in his late sixties, with a prominent belly and short stature, was walking around in a jockstrap, high-top shoes, and a tight-fitting tank top. By baseline cultural standards, this man could be considered unattractive—physically, he would traditionally be thought of as outside the paradigm of "sexy." The sexy standard we've all been fed for eons through the media still plays in the background (and foreground) of all our minds to some degree.

At a club with less of an open-door policy, he might have been ridiculed behind his back and left out of the fun play sessions happening around him. From all outward appearances, he didn't fit the demographic often seen as the gold standard of a "fun, sexy daddy." But what caught my eye was his energy and his absolute confidence that he belonged right where he was. He moved around the space with ease, and it was a delight to see him having fun. He gave off a subtle swagger that was both attractive and engaging.

There were other men there, of the same size and shape—men who, by societal standards, might be considered "unattractive." They stood on the sidelines, wearing heavy jeans, never making eye contact with anyone. They gave off a vibe of secrecy and almost shame. They seemed like they were just there to get what they could and leave quickly.

Both types of men were there for their own reasons, and both belonged—among the ever-present and adored gay Adonis types and the other various archetypes of queer men's appearances. This experience truly affirmed my belief in the energy we possess or embody when we're in spaces where, on some level, we are naked—whether literally or metaphorically. It really matters.

So, my theory is: What if there's something within us that opens up that part of ourselves that feels empowered and self-confident? How do we access that in the midst of overwhelming insecurity or imprints from our inherent unworthiness?

If we look inward and take stock of more than just what seems wrong or unfitting about ourselves, and instead focus on the parts of us that matter most, we may discover that we are much more than what the media portrays as acceptable or sexy. We all have parts of ourselves that *know* we're loved and seen. Our job is to remember it, rediscover it. This might require being generous and kind to our inner selves, looking toward what inspires us to embody our own inner swagger. Maybe you've had days or moments where you feel these qualities in yourself. Almost certainly, you've seen them in other people.

Years ago, when I was working in a restaurant, one of the servers, a woman named Colleen, was just about the funniest person I've ever known. She had this inner swagger. With her jokes, impersonations, funny observations, and uninhibited confidence, she cracked us up throughout the entire dinner shift. And here's the thing: On the nights she worked, everyone else was funnier too. The permission someone like Colleen gives to everyone around them is unmistakable. This kind of person embodies a generous, uplifting energy that makes everyone better. It was the same with the man at the sex club. Where he went and engaged, others followed suit. He was giving us all permission to access our own version of this inner swagger.

What inner energy are you accessing or embodying when you walk into the room? Finding our inner swagger calls us to get in touch with a sense of self-confidence, sexiness, and desirability. What happens when we seek out the sexier, smokier, sultrier, more deviant parts of ourselves? Can we see how this might feel empowering?

This type of energy can also be a source of safety and confidence for the person you're with. I know this from my experience with the men I've worked with over the years. They witness my self-assurance, which gives them permission to be self-assured as well. The mirroring that takes place is powerful, important, and much needed. This is one of the inner sanctums I've been able to create—a way to disarm the nervous insecurity or uncertainty that often arises when meeting someone for the first time. I've seen and felt the alchemy that happens between someone who offers that space and someone who is ready, willing, and able to step into it.

And it works both ways. I've had countless experiences where someone else's energy has resonated with me. It's almost like a rhythm—the rhythm of confidence. People who walk into a room appearing confident and aligned with their purpose are often great at conveying a message or telling a story. We often assume these are the people who have the handbook, the ones who have it all figured out. Yes, it's inspiring and attractive to see. Their energy draws people in and turns them on. This kind of person projects that energy in physical form to anyone there to experience it.

Then comes the shocker: We find out in conversation how insecure they were feeling when they arrived. Yet their honesty about those insecurities makes them even more real. Their own doubt and illusions of inadequacy were playing right alongside their inner swagger.

Does that lessen the fact that they radiate this energy? Do we hear that part of the story and suddenly discount their confident, inviting energy? I wouldn't think so. This permission-giving frequency says, "I am here! Where can I contribute?"

One of the ways I quell my anxious energy is to share my truth. I was at a naked pool party once and a lot of us were just standing around awkwardly—there seemed to be an uncomfortable energy. I finally said something to the effect of, "I have a lot of social anxiety right now, but I'm glad I'm here."

Guys began to chat me up, and someone even mentioned they were glad I said it because they too felt anxious. The rest of the party was great, even with the awkwardness that emerged from time to time.

What if we all have it in some form or another? What if it shows up for each of us in different ways? Finding that inner swagger can be challenging at times. Every time I walk into a room—both literally and figuratively—I try to ask myself: How can I be a safe harbor for the parts of myself that feel unseen and unwelcome? Am I meeting myself where I am? Can I be gentle with myself today? Who else is possible here? These are the times when I can cultivate the energy of knowing there is enough, that I *am* enough, and that whatever experience I'm about to encounter is a chance to discover more.

EXPLORING OUR FANTASIES

Do we consider our desires and inner dream states sacred? Are our fantasies meaningful? Or do we consider them merely a tool to assist us in an orgasm, like a launch fantasy? A great example of this is when we watch pornography or fantasize about a particular sexual scene or a favorite sexual act—something that gets us going and helps us launch our orgasm.

I love exploring fantasies in the Room of the Sacred. The reason is because I question whether we rarely share our fantasies with others because we see them as so deeply personal and private. Is it because they're so revered that we fear being shamed or rejected? Does it not align with our values that we live each day? The freedom of fantasy is that it doesn't have to match our beliefs or our ideas because it's rooted in ideas and sensory stimulation.

One of the elements that makes fantasy so interesting is that it can be a deeply personal, private, internal experience. I definitely want to get curious about why it feels so secretive, so personal. Maybe it's because the messages we received growing up brought a level of shame, or an element of taboo. Or maybe it's because these fantasies aren't things we actually want to act on in real life—they're just fantasies.

It's altogether too easy to get mixed up in what we think we're supposed to want—based on a lifetime of messaging from peers, parents, authority figures, society, and our own self-talk—and what we truly want. We may be tempted to see our fantasies as insignificant—maybe even downright unholy. So be it! Sometimes rebellion is the key to erotic freedom.

Some of our fantasies we keep to the realm of imagination. You might jerk off thinking about getting spanked, having an orgy, giving up all control, or dare I say a rape scene—which I don't mention casually, but it's not an uncommon submission fantasy. Within our fantasies, there may be other things we visualize might happen one day and that we would do if given the chance. We might even plan some out.

As a sex worker, I certainly have been the conductor of many well thought-out fantasies, gang bangs, and other fun experiences. Fantasies based in more dreamlike scenarios are valuable and absolutely sacred. They can exist anywhere on the spectrum—from vanilla to kinky—and be things we really want to things best kept in the realm of imagination. It's important to note that not everyone is a visual thinker. For some, fantasies don't appear in a visual way but more as emotional or experiential sensations. These fantasies are no less powerful or meaningful. Whether visual, emotional, or purely conceptual, they are part of the rich internal landscape that shapes our desires and gives us a sense of erotic freedom.

When exploring our fantasies, are there elements we feel embarrassed or ashamed of? Are there parts we've judged, and even more importantly, what's the possibility of allowing all of that into the Room of the Sacred—along with the understanding of how meaningful, important, and sacred our fantasies truly are?

If you were given a chance to make all your deepest, darkest, kinkiest fantasies come true, what would you experience? What would you want if you could wave a magic wand and have it? What would that look like?

I would be remiss not to mention fantasies that are harmful to the psyche or harmful to others in this section. There are indeed psychological phenomena that some struggle with, such as obsessive fantasizing about illegal activities. I cannot in good conscience explore that experience here. As I say throughout this book, if you feel that your fantasies border on self-harm, harm to others, or are dangerous and you may act on them, by all means, please utilize your support system. There is a great deal of help out there. I realize it can be difficult finding a trusted provider to carry your secret, but finding someone you can trust can be incredibly helpful.

THE SACRED HOOKUP

What if I said a one-time encounter can be just as sacred as an ongoing sexual connection? What if some of us cultivate trust and vulnerability at different speeds?

I think we can all agree that sexual intimacy of any kind can be deeply meaningful and play a crucial role in our overall health and wellness.

As a sex worker, I always tried to cultivate a connection with each of the men I worked with because it was a vital part of my work. Outside of work, however, my sexual experiences have spanned the entire spectrum—from those with deep emotional attachment to anonymous, random sex. I can tell you that the potential for a highly meaningful sexual interaction in a one-time anonymous encounter is just as possible, and just as sacred, as anything else in my sex life.

Casual hookups are easy targets for criticism, often labeled unhealthy through a very heteronormative lens of sex. The pathologizing of sexual exploration is as old as the Dark Ages. In queer culture, it's not uncommon for men to engage in casual encounters, often facilitated by a brief interaction on an app, a dating site, or an in-person connection at a bar, on the street, or anywhere. One of the objectives of these interactions is a sexual connection, whether short-term, long-term, or both.

Sometimes we just need to be touched and to find connection, and for queer men, that can happen in many ways. Yes, dating and getting to know a partner is viable and important, but what happens when we get into the room and have no experience reading cues and desires? We may be caught up in our own inner dialogue—"Am I good in bed?" or "What if they don't enjoy this?" I think many people just make do with what they know, which is often influenced by a mix of complex past experiences or what we've seen in porn. If we've spent years limiting ourselves, hidden behind the walls we built when we got hurt, or haven't explored ways to connect intimately with others, it can be a very frightening endeavor.

Well, I have good news: what if there's a way to cultivate your intuitive ability to connect with others sexually and otherwise? To get there, let me digress a bit about why I believe a one-time hookup can be just as sacred and empowering as more complex experiences.

Many years ago, I used to frequent Lands End, a beach in San Francisco known for cruising. One day, I walked past a man sitting on the rocks. I glanced back, and he gave me an energetic invitation—a kind of mental telepathy embedded in all gay men of that time. Of course, we have to tune into it, but that's the art of cruising. It's mostly about body language and energy, with very few words exchanged.

Now, to an outside observer, it might seem like there was no connection, no conversation, no "getting to know each other." But I say that's not true. We were both there for the same reason—seeking sexual touch and gratification. We both understood that, and the rest we worked out on our own. He led me to a hidden spot, and we started kissing and playing. We took turns blowing each other. We both were passionate and deeply connected. Of course, we kept one eye out for people approaching—even though anyone on that foggy, 63-degree beach was likely there for the same reason and might have even been invited to join.

That said, we didn't need to know each other's politics or professions. We didn't need to dive into what we had in common. We accepted each other right there, at that moment—two men looking for a connection. And we provided that for each other, free of judgment. We found our common ground, touched each other, and parted ways. As I walked back, I enjoyed the brief erotic connection and the feeling of pure acceptance we had shared.

Our culture has taught us to keep a list of what we want from a partner or a friend. It teaches us that relationships, built through inquiry and shared traits and beliefs, are the conduit to this idea of a "true" connection—often with the goal of finding "The One." And yes, for some, that may be true. But there's something magical about meeting someone right where they are and finding refuge in a fun, hot time. It builds esteem when seen as healthy.

What confuses many is that this type of connection is often viewed as compulsive or needy—born from a sense of lack or desperation. Even if that's true sometimes, on some level, it's still healthy sexual behavior. Two humans bonding, meeting each other's needs—physical, intimate, and emotional. There's much more going on in the body and soul during a connected touch. The relief and passion that take place are beautiful and affirming. It quells loneliness and validates each other. Even if only for a short while. What if the effect is cumulative and empowering (it certainly was for me)—and yes, dare I say, sacred.

The LGBTQIA+2 community is rife with debates about the nature of hookups. Some argue these interactions are shallow, disconnected, or detrimental to health. While hooking up may not be for everyone, I stand by the assertion that even the most casual encounter can forge a meaningful connection, however fleeting. These experiences teach us how to connect in the moment. They remind us that the judgments and ideas keeping us locked in sexual stalemates can be broken free.

I have a whole history of encounters with the men I have worked with, where we've shared revelatory, life-long memory-making sexual experiences. Some report back that their marriages or relationships have grown stronger. The same goes for my fuckbuddies—of which I have many. These experiences provide us with vital knowledge that carries into our lives.

Gratification and the sexual empowerment of a hookup is a wonderful place to practice sexual freedom. I haven't talked enough in this book about practice, so let me say it now: Practice, practice, practice. Fall down, fail, get rejected, feel embarrassed and uncomfortable, get weird and awkward—because your inner swagger is going to show up right alongside all the chaos that comes with exploring your sexual wellbeing. And you might just look over one evening and realize you're having the time of your life.

There are heaps of sober sex parties and play groups that are inviting and inclusive. While casual encounters might be terrifying, they can also be earth-shatteringly informative. Historically, and still today in many places around the world, queer people have had to meet in parks, in secret. Because these encounters were fleeting, a lot needed to be accomplished in a short time. Yes, it's scary and unfamiliar to some. Imagine navigating consent essentially through body language and energy. That's what we did at the beach—that's what we had to do. It was a kind of mental telepathy, awkwardly signaling our needs with hankie codes and our outward appearances.

We can pine for those days, but we can also revel in the parts that have returned because sexual freedom is experiencing a bit of a renaissance right now. And we can dive headfirst into the new digital back alleys.

If you're exploring, there's so much to discover on the great adventure of sex, love, and intimacy.

Say yes to getting dressed up in leather or some fun gear and heading out for the night. Say yes to going camping with a group of bears or joining a puppy mosh. Find your pack where you can. We're looking for you.

TAKING RISKS

Let's go deeper—and possibly even scarier now. What's it like to do what absolutely every fiber of your being resists? The paralyzing fear of asking for what you want. The idea that what you desire is somehow not worthy of acceptance or embrace.

In what way does this happen for you? What would a risk look like for you? Where is your edge? You might expect this chapter to explore high-risk sexual behavior—it's a predictable angle on risk-taking, and certainly, that can be part of our lives as sexual beings. But I'm talking about the emotional risk of asking for what we want sexually. It means being vulnerable and sharing ourselves in what might be a new way.

A lot of the time, this is a battle we wage against the belief that our desires aren't valid, that we don't deserve whatever it is we're asking for—or not asking for. I saw this in my work all the time.

This dynamic plays out across the entire spectrum of experiences. Sometimes, for some, it's much easier to ask an anonymous partner or a sex worker for what we want than to ask a long-term partner. We think we already know how they would respond. Men often share with me their struggles in the intimacy department and their hesitation to rekindle physical and emotional closeness with their partners. I'll often ask, "When was the last time you asked for intimacy? When did you last engage in a face-to-face, vulnerable conversation to invite erotic play?"

For many, those kinds of questions—simple on the surface but complicated in practice—represent a high level of reluctance, and therefore, risk. It can be difficult to return to physical intimacy in a relationship where it's dropped away, where not having sex becomes the norm. Many men accept the idea that the intimacy they get from companionship with the one person they can trust is enough for them. Although some believe it's too late to get it back, often, our "risk muscle" just needs strengthening. That starts with taking small risks, planning gentle nudges to proactively go after an outcome we desire.

It's important to make sure the risks you choose come with a reasonable chance of success. Otherwise, we're just chasing down confirmation of our own illusions of inadequacy. Put another way: Don't let your desire define you. Don't go after something because you think you need it to be made whole, affirmed, or validated. Go after it because you want it—because it springs from your own sacred desires.

If we have skillfully avoided taking risks—such as asking for what we want because we're too afraid to be transparent about our desires—we risk falling into isolation, separation, and loneliness, if we're not there already. I'm not saying any of this is easy. It's difficult for everyone.

Let's start with some self inquiry:

What are some risks you've thought about taking, but haven't?

When and where do you hesitate to voice your desire?

What makes you play small?

Is there a declared reason for not taking said risk, some name tag or "I am" statement that stands in the way? I am too fat, I am too old he won't understand this at all.

When it comes to genuine desire and fantasy—those experiences we're eager to try—we often hesitate to voice them because we're trapped in a state of insecurity, fear, or both.

Many of us, myself included, struggle with asking for what we want. A lot of this fear or reluctance is based on the belief that what we want doesn't matter or that it's only meaningful or important to us. *What if I ask for something he doesn't want to give? What if he judges me for my request? What if I don't get what I want?* Or even scarier: *What if I do get what I want?!*

As you contemplate your answers to this, consider taking some well calculated risks. Look for opportunities to push past that edge of resistance. This kind of risk is inherent and necessary as you excavate your sense of sexual freedom. Some kind of breaking through might be essential

Start small, if that helps. Lower the challenge level for yourself. For those with the resources and inclination, that may mean getting a massage or engaging the services of a trusted sex worker. Putting yourself into the position of a paid client can make it easier to ask for what you want. If that isn't accessible to you, I'm a huge fan of massage exchange groups, hosted by organizations around the globe. Not only is it incredibly gratifying and healthy to be touched, but many of these groups practice the art of asking for what we want. You'll find resources in the appendices of this book on where to find some of these groups.

In any case, be intentional about it. Communicate your needs and desires openly and honestly, even if it feels uncomfortable.

When you're ready, reach out to someone you want to engage with. Initiating contact requires courage. (Note: By no means is this an invitation to set ourselves up for rejection. Be aware of your emotional well-being and nurture yourself before taking risks that involve high chances of rejection.)

Maybe the object of your request is a familiar or long-term partner. This doesn't necessarily make it any easier, especially if you've fallen out of practice. By taking these emotional risks, we open the door to deeper connections and new experiences that can enrich our lives.

And by the way, none of this comes with any guarantee. That's part of the risk—and even part of the payoff. You may not get the reaction you're looking for, and you may not get the action you're looking for, either. If so, try to practice some of the noticing and allowing that The Four Rooms incorporates elsewhere. We all need practice with these things—including practice with rejection. Don't let that define you any more than your thoughts, emotions, or body defines you.

The Stoic philosopher Lucius Annaeus Seneca once said, "It is not because things are difficult that we do not dare; it is because we do not dare that they are difficult." Going after something you feel you need might make taking the risk more intense, as opposed to going after something you want.

If it's a want, then you're more likely to feel okay about not getting it. If it's a need, not getting it can be demoralizing. Operating from a place of empowerment and courage can be less challenging.

Ask yourself whether you can embrace that you want whatever it is (the attention of another man, getting laid, finding a boyfriend, having a date go well, or even just getting deep-dicked) without attributing so much power to it—so much need—that you feel defined by whether or not you get it.

Remember the bungee jump story: We may feel dread and fear every single time, but right alongside that is a version of us we're reintroducing. We won't be the cock of the walk on the first jump, maybe not even the first five jumps, but we will gather more information about how we can do hard things without embodying the parts of us that want to steal the spotlight. Jump, I say! Hire a sex worker or get a massage. Exploring BDSM can be highly freeing. This could also be a great time to have a deeper conversation with your current partner or partners about shifting some of your desires. The sky's the limit.

As with everything else in this book, your mileage may vary. For some, a next-step risk might be asking your partner for physical cuddling, to fuck you, or if you can fuck them. You might want them to be more communicative about sex. For others, that risk might mean getting out of the house, going to a bar, or hopping online to see who and what is out there. For someone else, it might mean going to a bathhouse or a sex party, engaging in anonymous encounters you've been close to trying but haven't yet found the gumption to pursue. Maybe it's just taking yourself out on a date. Whatever the risk is—take the risk.

Your desire is worth pursuing. If we are too invested in our imprints and the messages we get from the world that our desire is not sacred, not important, not worthy, we risk letting that play out in our conscious or subconscious minds—probably both. Even as we pursue our desires, we can ask ourselves where to allow those thoughts and feelings without letting them take up all the space in the room. How can we make room for more possibilities and allow our risks, rejections, and explorations to not bury us in the rubble?

SEXUAL VALUES

Let's explore our sexual values in the same way we would our traditional values, such as honesty, integrity, and so on. Your sexual values are your internal compass, guiding your behavior, decisions, and actions. They will evolve and change, so flexibility will be important.

What are your sexual values? Take some time to reflect on these or write down your thoughts. Consider what your relationship deal-breakers are. For example, you might not want to date someone with violent tendencies or someone who treats others poorly.

Maybe you aren't into monogamy and don't want to limit your sexual life to one person. Or perhaps you desire monogamy, or something in between. What is nonnegotiable for you? It could be manipulation, lying, distrust, disrespect, belittling, or gaslighting.

What makes a sexual experience meaningful for you? Maybe it's open communication, intimacy, honesty, or the ability to really be in touch with your feelings and convey them in a way that feels safe for both of you.

Think back on your most memorable sexual experiences—what conditions were present? Maybe there was a combination of intensity and caring, some verbal role play, or even a warm embrace. Maybe there great aftercare, a fun, joking atmosphere or deep conversations about how much you enjoyed yourselves.

Was communication easy—were you able to ask for what you wanted and were they able to ask for what they wanted?

Identifying these things can be useful—not just so we can more clearly go after what we want, but so that we can recognize when we're aligned with our values and when we're not. And as always, you may have more than one answer to these kinds of questions—and they might even contradict each other.

For instance, you might consider anonymous sex one of your deal-breakers. You may believe you need to know and like someone before getting naked with them. But at the same time, you cherish that formative experience with the hot stranger in the gym showers—the guy whose name you never learned but who you'll never forget. You could even be perfectly at home in a hotel room, having anonymous hookups every few weeks as part of your sexual self-care. Believe me, I know many slutty boys who do this, and I absolutely get it.

There are people who will scoff and cry out about sexual compulsion and the supposed dangers of this type of value system. But I say hogwash. It's the judgment, learned ideology, and societal droning of sex as a pathology that keeps these myths alive. Most sexually active guys who explore in this way know their limits and are usually pretty good at keeping themselves safe. Of course, there are exceptions, and we fear this because those are the stories that tend to make the rounds. People love a good tragedy. It's odd, but like a car wreck, we tend not to be able to look away.

It is often judgment that creates a misaligned values system, which rarely cultivates anything but shame. Remaining curious is a great way to find your sexual values. Yucking someone else's yum is rarely the foundation for formulating sexual values. Instead, finding your rhythm in areas you connect with and enjoy—deciding that you want more of one thing and less of another—can help you develop a more authentic sense of your sexual values. And this, once again, involves practice!

A great deal of sex workers spend so much time giving, being in control, and showing up for the the men they see in ways that can sometimes feel one-sided. In my experience, being a top is 99% of my work when the clothes come off. So, when I want to balance myself out, I tend to bottom in my personal time because I need to receive and recharge my batteries. That, of course, is not the case for everyone, but for me, it's an important part of my sexual values—being balanced and sexually healthy so I have the bandwidth to show up and give 100 percent to the men I work with. There's room for all of it.

So, what are the principles and beliefs that guide your choices and actions? What values are sacred to you? For myself, in my personal daily life, one of my values is to always leave behind a trail of generosity and kindness, to the best of my ability. Does this mean everyone I've ever met will remember me this way? Of course not. Please remember that this is about ideals, not about living perfectly by those ideals all the time.

Other examples of sexual values might include consent, self-respect, communication, personal choice, honesty, or loyalty. Ask yourself whether your values and desires around sex bring joy, pleasure, and fulfillment.

THE PERFECT PARTNER

The perfect partner experience is a fantastic way to uncover a few of your sexual values. I created this workshop years ago, and I still use it because it has such a powerful impact on people. It would be a shame not to include it here. So, grab a notebook.

First, think about what you truly want in a relationship. Be honest with yourself. Do you believe in monogamy, or are you somewhere on the spectrum that includes polyamory? Some people have a "don't ask, don't tell" policy, while others are absolutely not OK with that. These are deeply personal questions, and everyone has different answers.

Now, pretend you've been in the perfect relationship—whatever that means for you—for the past five years. This is where you need to suspend reality for a moment. Don't use any current or past relationships as a template—instead, start from scratch. Now, write a gratitude letter to your perfect partner(s), detailing all the things you're grateful for and all the ways they fill you up.

Set your timer for fifteen minutes and just start writing. When you're done, sign it, and go on with your day. Be bold. Be creative. Have fun.

If you want to write your letter from scratch or record a voice memo on your phone, absolutely go for it. It's up to you! If you'd like a little guidance, here's a template you can work from.

Dear "Perfect Partner" _____

I want to take a few moments today to express how grateful I am to have you in my life.

This journey has been so very _____

I want to thank you for always _____

I want you to know that I am _____

I love it when we can _____ and

_____

_____

You have so many incredible qualities I love _____

_____

and the times when you _____

_____

You are safe to be with I always want you to know that I will _____

_____

_____

When we are aligned nothing can _____

_____

You are_____

_____

and I want you to know that I love you even when _____

_____

_____

I love our _____

_____

I will always be _____

_____

Thank you for _____

_____

_____

Love, _____

Once you've had some time and distance—whether the next day or even next week—read your gratitude letter aloud to yourself. Only this time, put your name at the top as if your perfect partner wrote it for you.

How much of it applies to you? What does it reveal about your desires and sexual values? This exercise peels back the layers, revealing not only your preferences and attractions but also the dynamics of how you want to be treated and how you derive pleasure in treating your intimate partners.

The real question is: Can we live up to the expectations and desires we hold others to? Are we judging ourselves for having unrealistic expectations of others?

I've had people come up to me in grocery stores or at other events telling me they attended one of my workshops where we did this exercise, and that they redo this letter every year. Some record it on their phones, listen to it being read back to themselves, or even create meditations out of their letter with music in the background. It's a powerful exercise. I hope you get creative with it, too.

TAKING STOCK OF THE SACRED

The Room of the Sacred has many moving parts. The point I'm cultivating here is that when we reaffirm all the things that are meaningful to us, and begin gathering the sacred elements to fill this room, the room gets bigger. Our hearts get bigger. The stage where all our insecurities dance expands, giving us more space to pay attention to the areas where we flourish. The spotlight doesn't always need to be on the parts of ourselves that feel "less than" or "not enough." Instead, the dance includes what's working and what we hold sacred.

We don't need to export our prayers, hopes, and dreams to some mysterious light source "out there"—unless we choose to—because it's rooted within us, created by how we live in the world. Not just in our sex lives, but in how we embody our values and ideas, which form the foundation of our self-worth and create a trusting, abiding sense of safety. This allows us to explore who we are and what other possibilities exist in the present moment.

Once we take stock of everything we enjoy and appreciate, we recognize these as our most cherished treasures. These treasures are found when we realize where we've been, when we embrace the wisdom of our deepest, darkest desires, and when we muster the courage to see the path forward.

We often read inspiring and motivational books. And we are flooded with encouraging memes and positive "YOU CAN DO IT" quotes online. But I don't need to do that here. Once you have furnished the Room of the Sacred, you can sit and just *be* in it, knowing that neither the temple on the mountain nor the dogma in the great books has anything on the sacred temple you uncover in your world each day.

This isn't a "stop and smell the roses" moment—it's a call to action. It's time to truly look around.

SEXUAL AWARENESS IN*QUEER*Y

Let's take another inventory of our sexual experiences in The Room of the Sacred. Remember, there are no right or wrong answers—simply consider these questions and see what comes up. If you like, use a journal to note any thoughts or feelings.

Reflect on the last time you had an orgasm or engaged in sexual pleasure. This could include self-pleasure, a hookup, cruising on the street, a scheduled sex-work appointment (massage, escort, live cam show, etc.), online sexting, sex with a partner, etc.

What stands out about this experience? Did it feel meaningful or sacred, or did it seem compulsive or unhealthy? What made you feel that way? It's OK if you can't remember the details.

Do you have a favorite way to get off, such as watching porn, fantasizing, using toys, getting blow jobs, jacking off, getting penetrated, etc.? Do you feel any judgment about your preferences?

Reflect on the last time you felt truly connected—either with yourself or your partner(s). What made that moment special? In what ways do you see your sex life as sacred?

Throughout your day and the week ahead, remember to practice asking empowering questions—and to live in those questions rather than try to answer them. Allow ideas and answers to arrive on their own. Your role is simply to observe and gather insights you can use.

THE BODY

THE ROOM OF THE BODY

For almost two decades, I have crossed the thresholds of rooms where the men I work with have some of the most complicated relationships with their bodies. It's a risk, but I'll say it anyway: many are not even present in their own bodies. They exited long ago, most likely at the moment of what Don Miguel Ruiz, in *The Four Agreements*, calls "our domestication."

In other words, the breaking of the spirit. It's the moment we disconnect from our essential selves—usually when we are very young or have experienced some personal cataclysmic trauma. The message isn't that we were bad or that what we did was wrong. It's usually delivered with shame, oppression, and a clear judgment that who we are is wrong, unworthy, and unacceptable.

Because of my own experience, at a very young age, with this severing of my spirit from my essential self and the construction of a version of myself based on survival and fear, I'm able to show up for these men. I don't really know how to describe it authentically because I don't fully understand it myself. The best I can conjure is an unspoken knowingness that communicates and mirrors a sense of identification, which, for lack of a better term, I can only describe as a sort of energetic alchemy. It allows me to be relatable and disarming. This is not intentional, nor is it a practiced skill. Sometimes, trust arrives immediately; other times, it's more subtle and slower. But it arrives, and I can see them for who they are in that moment—and beyond.

Growing up severely abused, rejected, and cast out by my parents, my peers, and even myself—as I later reinforced my own beliefs about my worthiness, drowning in alcohol and drug addiction—I was steeped in shame throughout much of my childhood and into adulthood. My healing was long and difficult, much of it happening before I could fully inhabit my own body. Armed with this lived experience, I've found I can show up for men who feel absolutely unacceptable, too.

I have walked into rooms with men who haven't dared to look at themselves, except with disdain and disgust, because that's what the world modeled to them. The body of a 500-hundred-pound man, covered in scabs and painful skin diseases, who has never known a moment of peace and has rarely felt the touch of true intimacy and connection. There are hundreds of examples—of those I have stood with in the face of absolute self-loathing. As well as those who don't have any outward appearances that would tell such a tale. I see it. I know it on such a deep level that I can only conclude the body truly holds all that we believe we are. It is why I am so passionate about touch and acceptance, and why I am so profoundly grateful to be given the gift of trust from these men.

Nearly all I believe about sex, love, and intimacy, I learned from those who rarely ever experienced it. Their bodies—their whole beings and all they carried—shared this wisdom with me, again and again. So when I write about the body, I'm not just speaking about the physical form. This is why the body is the fourth room, not the first or second. It embodies all the rooms and experiences combined.

The body is not just a physical entity but a vessel for emotional, psychological, and sacred experiences. It experiences everything: your imprint, your beliefs, your perceived self-worth, your orgasms, your heartbreak. It constantly measures your worth in comparison to others. It experiences ecstasy and your resistance to ecstasy, and it documents your traumas and victories. The body is where so much of what we've been discussing lives—the thinking mind, the emotions, the sacredness of our world, and yes, the act of getting off. Everything we experience resides in the body.

You might wonder how emotions and thoughts find a home in the physical realm of our bodies. Modern neurology gives us a window into how this all works. Emotions aren't just some abstract energy—they set off real, physical responses. When you feel happiness, for instance, dopamine and serotonin surge through your system—the "feel-good" neurotransmitters. But when faced with a threat, adrenaline kicks in, and that's when you get the classic "fight, flight, freeze, or fawn" response. These chemical reactions show us just how connected our emotions are to what's happening in our bodies.

But while the neurochemical side of emotions is fascinating, it's only part of the story. Layered on top of this are the judgments—the thoughts and beliefs we adopt as part of ourselves. Like inscriptions carved into the walls of a temple, our judgments leave their mark on our psyche. Each self-critique or opinion about others adds another chapter to the story written within our body.

We could easily get into the weeds about how judging others can activate our dopamine, making us feel powerful or validated. After all, judgment can trigger "feel-good" chemicals too. But do we really need to investigate that further? We already know what it feels like to be judged. Is the payoff worth the pain it inflicts on someone else? I'm not sure it is. And what about when we feel shame, rejection, or our own regret and remorse? There's no escaping the emotional residue that lives in our bodies, so I'll leave it at that.

The body as a vessel for our cognitive and emotional experiences is a concept explored by various authors, thinkers, and philosophers across different fields and contexts. Some well-known examples include Eckhart Tolle's idea of the "pain body," which he says is the source of our negative emotions; psychiatrist Bessel van der Kolk's work on how trauma physically shows up in the body; neuroscientist Candace Pert's research into how emotions are actually rooted in our biology; and Zen Buddhist monk Thich Nhat Hanh's teachings on "mindfulness of the body" as a path to emotional well-being.

Each of these authors brings something useful to the table. But when it comes to sexual freedom and well-being—especially for queer men—there's a lot more to consider. No philosopher without layers of queer experience can speak to the unique challenges our community faces. Walking through a bathhouse, feeling ridiculous and ugly, carrying all the nerve-wracking feelings of not-enoughness and insecurity, while wondering what mystery might be around the corner of a dark hallway. Most people can't even fathom the heavy weight of societal judgment about our very existence—whether in the pharmacy, the court system, our own family living rooms, or right there in the sex club. Nobody else can prescribe a narrative that will save us from the imprints and deeply stored ideas we carry about our self-worth

The self-help world is full of affirmations, meditations, and quick-fix solutions. That might work for some, but in the end, the real expert on your body is you. Nobody knows what your body knows.

There's a lot to unpack, including our own judgments and biases. The journey ahead is ours to take. So let's keep going.

QUEER BODY CULTURE

Let's start by looking at our physical bodies and explore the standards we often hold ourselves to. Society, the medical industry, our culture, media, and digital platforms constantly bombard us with benchmarks for an "ideal" body—what's acceptable and what's not. These standards may have shifted over time, but the pressure to conform—to whatever the current norm may be—remains.

As queer people, we've often had complicated relationships with our bodies, with added layers of cultural battles we've witnessed or been part of along the way. Many in our community compare their bodies to others. While that can happen to anyone, queer men are disproportionately impacted by it.

There are real consequences that come from the collective issues of believing our bodies are too much or not enough. We're almost always in view of a message that says, "My body doesn't look like that body." Those influences and imprints become the template we feel we need to journey toward. Suddenly, we have a problem that needs a solution. We might push ourselves into intense diets, grueling workouts, cycles of steroids, or—for those privileged enough—surgeries, all in an effort to obtain that perfect body. And often, no matter how strong or beautiful or "perfect" we become, it's still not enough.

Others may do nothing, feeling insurmountable waves of disappointment in being in the body they live in. We're bombarded with the notion that our bodies must conform to a certain standard of beauty to fit into the spaces, places, and hearts we desire.

Those without access to expensive foods, gym memberships, or "clean" diets often find themselves on the margins, receiving ableist feedback loops telling them they need to change. "Eat better," "lose weight," "get out there and meet the world head-on"—all supposedly for their own good. There's no end to the insufferable advisors who are blind to the reality that some people face unseen and unheard challenges. Being ostracized or made invisible because of their body, age, race, or gender barely scratches the surface of what they're experiencing.

In the Room of the Body, I want to honor the diversity of queer men and challenge the archetype of the fit, gay, white male as the sole standard of beauty. If you're a person of color trying to navigate the racism in white queer culture, bring that into the room. If you identify as anything other than the G in LGBTQIA+2, bring that too. If your body doesn't look like the guys in the underwear ads, I invite you to bring that. If you face income or healthcare barriers, I acknowledge and welcome you. I want to make the room big enough for all of us and all parts of us. You don't need to fit in—you belong just by being who you are.

Many queer communities have subcultures, each with their own body ideals. Whether bears, twinks, fems, daddies, or muscle bears, we label (name tag) ourselves, longing to find our place beneath the LGBTQIA+2 umbrella. For those of us who struggle with body image, we may conclude we don't fit into any of those boxes, reaffirming once again our sense of not belonging.

This ever-present sense of not-enoughness doesn't spare even the most classically attractive. A stereotypical Adonis may be admired and accepted, yet still feel like they don't fit in. These illusions of inadequacy run rampant through our queer culture. And though society seems to be evolving, for many of us, it feels like one step forward, two steps back.

This brings to mind trans and nonbinary people, who live in a society steeped in judgment and dogma around gender expression. There's inescapable trauma for gender nonconforming people who are constantly under attack, both from within and outside our community—an ongoing cultivation of disdain. As we speak, hundreds of bills in the USA are targeting trans and gender nonconforming people. Yet, many allies remain silent, unaware that the ignorance flowing freely throughout the country will absolutely impact them too. We know that speaking up, holding space, and being courageous is required right now. Trans bodies are being attacked, and their personhood is dehumanized daily.

As I mentioned earlier—and it bears repeating—the farther we are from the paradigm of cis, able-bodied, white, hetero-passing, masculine-presenting, the more layers of un-belonging we experience. Nearly everyone struggles with their relationship to their body. Really think about that: queer folx don't have a monopoly on being at odds with their bodies, but we are in near-constant awareness of it.

Before we dive deeper into the Room of the Body, I want to remind us that we're not here to change the way we feel about our bodies or convince ourselves they're acceptable and perfect as they are. We're here to make room for our bodies and all they carry. So, gather your grace, knowing our queer bodies are immersed in generational traumas and that our confusion and desire to push away from what we see in the mirror is neither surprising nor unusual, no matter what shape we're in.

WHOLENESS IN THE BODY

What if, for a moment, we set aside critiques and comparisons and simply existed within our bodies? Felt the rhythm of our heartbeat, the depth of our breath, the sheer vitality coursing through our veins? Would that presence redefine our relationship with our physical selves? Maybe, maybe not. This is about possibility, not certainty—no guarantees, no preconditions for cultivating the curiosity, awareness, and perspective I've been talking about all along.

What if we moved forward with the sex lives we imagine for ourselves and recognized that our bodies are the empowering vehicles that get us there? What would it be like to fully live in our whole body, to experience ourselves completely?

When I think about sexual freedom, I picture myself living in one big room where everything I feel, think, and do is welcomed—allowed to exist in the experience. This is the hard part to express clearly, but the key I'm trying to convey is that this isn't about eliminating suffering or erasing your history. It's about stepping back, looking around, and realizing it was all one room the whole time.

When we're naked in the room, all the rooms are present. It's our resistance, our need to rearrange the furniture, that distracts us or keeps us from fully showing up. This is where connection, disconnection, and, of course, the getting off happens. There's physical tension and release, but also thoughts, feelings, awkwardness, imprints, and that not-enoughness—all experienced in the body.

This wholeness reaffirms the idea that everything—my thoughts, ideas, beliefs, inadequacies, anxieties, joy, even my eroticism—belongs in the whole house. Not isolated rooms having compartmentalized experiences, but one big, integrated space. You are a complete being, and every part of you is sacred, valued, and worthy. I know how that might sound—as though I'm suggesting we're all perfect beings capable of perfect happiness if only we can figure it out. But that's not what I'm saying.

What I mean is: You are perfectly who you are. The more you allow yourself to just be—with your thoughts, emotions, desires—the more information you have to work with. Being present with all parts of yourself is no easy task. You may have versions of yourself that are still in exile, parts you resist. And so be it. The important thing is to become aware of the parts of you that you can be with right now.

What if, instead of trying to fix everything we dislike about our bodies, we allowed the parts of us that are working to shine? Wholeness isn't about accepting everything all the time—it's about noticing who we are in that moment and making room for it. Even if your inner critic shows up and wants to be the loudest voice in the room, notice it. Let it speak, and then get curious about it. You might find you're exactly the person someone needs to see.

What would it be like to stand naked in front of a mirror and fully experience your body? To stand with your imprints, insecurities, your not-enoughness—all of it—right alongside what's working for you? How would it feel to see your body in this moment, without needing to change anything about it?

In what ways are you grateful for your body? What would it be like to just *be* in your body right now? What parts of your body make you uncomfortable?

If seeing your body makes you uncomfortable, allow yourself to be curious about that. Can you become a witness to your physical body? Are you hyper-focused on flaws, on the fat or the scar? Or can you create space for what else might be possible, beyond what you've always known? What else exists in this room? Can you make the room bigger for more possibilities without needing to shed the insecurity or anxiety? What else is available to you in this experience? What's right in front of you—such as your excitement or sexual craving—that the shadows have shielded from view? What's available to you that you haven't noticed yet?

When we're in the room, it's all there anyway. It just might take some getting used to. Every time you look at yourself, you're not just seeing a physical form. You're also seeing everything you make of that image—the internal dialogue and every societal standard that's been subtly or overtly imposed on us. The way we see our bodies can feel overwhelming because of the experiences we've had related to them. How we view ourselves and our bodies can shift from day to day, influenced by our mood, circumstances, and whatever else might come up in those cycles.

Try this with me right now: Close your eyes, and do a quick mental scan of your body. Start at the crown of your head and work down through your neck, shoulders, arms, chest, midsection, ass, crotch, legs, and feet. Just sit and relax, breathing normally and easily.

If it's possible, when you're ready, get completely naked and stand in front of the mirror. Explore your body, just like in the scan with your eyes closed. Thoughts? Notice them. Feelings? Allow them. Demand nothing of them except that they allow you to witness them.

As you are witnessing them, what do you see? Is there judgment or criticism? Is there an inner conversation happening? What parts of your body do you criticize the most? Are there specific regions that invoke the most potent emotions? What happens as you get to each region of the body? What messages arrive? Maybe there are stories, judgments, or feelings there may even be a sense of elation or gratitude, kindness and acceptance.

It's perfectly fine—and absolutely 100 percent acceptable—to feel a bit distracted, disconnected, even destabilized. The trick is to experience a bit at a time. Give yourself some grace. Take short breaks or return later to the mirror just to observe. When judgment arrives, remember: you're not here to get this "right." There is no "wrong" way to get into the Room of the Body.

Each sensation offers insight into the narratives we've constructed or inherited about our bodies. But that doesn't mean we have to endure an avalanche of despair—again, this is not the gym. None of this is about shedding ourselves of judgment. It's not about making our perceived limitations—or those of our potential sexual partners—invisible.

When I spend time with the men I see, each of whom brings his own collection of ideas and issues into the room, I try to embody a sense of presence and wholeness. Yes, I'm aware of the struggles they tell me about or show me by default. I see the fat. I see the scars. I notice the fear and their sense of inadequacy. I'm never going to say those things don't exist. I'm going to get curious about what that means for us and how we, together, can allow it to sit on the sidelines while we fuck our brains out.

We get to be witnesses and observers of the limits and ideas that may block us from the sexual connection we desire, but what if we allowed the very thing we struggle with to sit at the table? Like a less-than-welcome family member coming to dinner for the holidays. Can you pull up a chair for the guest you have a difficult relationship with while chatting up the ones you're actually there to see?

Imagine being unbothered by that one family member who annoys you, while still living your best life right in front of them. That energy is powerful. It's rebellious. It's standing in your power in the face of the fat, or the idea that your cock isn't big enough, or any of the insecurities that want to suck the air out of the room rather than let you suck something more enjoyable.

One of the things I hope you'll allow is graciousness in your view of the entire picture. We don't sneer across the table at our undesirable guests. We give a kind nod, being polite, acknowledging that their presence has value and wisdom to offer.

This journey most likely won't be a straight line. I'd even venture to say it's not even close. There's a very real chance that sliding back into old patterns, or losing some of our illusion of inadequacy only to have it come roaring back on any given day, is completely normal and to be expected. It's our judgment and expectation of a cure that gets us into the weeds.

Once we've explored, experienced, and made the room bigger, I can't promise the room will never shrink again. But even then, it will happen in a new context of its own.

Oliver Wendell Holmes said, "A man's mind, stretched by new ideas, may never return to its original dimensions." I'm not sure I fully agree, but I know on some levels, as our relationship to these dreaded yet divine roadblocks and insecurities shifts, so will our experiences of them.

DIEGO'S STORY

I met Diego during the Four Rooms beta course, a four-week online group I created to gather data for this book.

Diego was injured in a traffic accident while crossing the street as a young child and became a quadriplegic. As he grew into adolescence and adulthood, his desire for sex and the discovery of his sexuality emerged. Given that he was an avid Roman Catholic and preparing for his first holy Communion, the shame and sense of wrongness showed up, too.

Imagine not being able to reach out and touch your partner or express yourself physically during a sexual encounter. Knowing the teachings of the church, Diego started praying for God to remove his homosexuality. It wasn't until a registered nurse introduced him to a massage therapist who offered him a happy ending that Diego experienced sexual relief. This act of connection opened the door for him to begin exploring his desires.

The fact is, Diego still has all his erotic senses. He has feeling in his body, can get an erection, and can ejaculate—something he feels fortunate about. He's found ways to use his imagination and connect with his sexual partners.

I asked Diego, "What do you struggle with the most?" He said, "I want to please my partner, and not being able to touch or physically give to my partner makes me feel like I'm not doing my part. In my mind, I imagined sex one way—what I knew from able-bodied sex in porn and pop culture. I believed I was incapable of giving him what he needs, even though I've done a lot of work on this. It's still a struggle for me to feel like I'm fully part of the experience."

Diego clearly had belief systems and imprints about what sex was supposed to look like. We can all refer to our lists of influences in our able-bodied world to find the origins of this struggle. But Diego has learned to make room for sexual experiences—ones he used to think were impossible for him—alongside the emotional and physical imprints and obstacles.

On an intuitive level, Diego has come to understand that we are more than our beliefs, emotions, or bodies. He participated in the group all four weeks, inspiring us and teaching us things we might not have considered part of a sexual freedom template—things that were specific to him but relatable to us all. His journey was different, but his struggles were on par with our online group experiment.

Many of the workshop exercises were written before Diego signed up, but having his contributions in the Room of the Body was imperative. Diego is preparing to do a TEDx talk on normalizing sex and being free of shame, and I can't wait to see what more comes from his world.

THE EROTIC BODY

I've been with hundreds of men. I know how to kiss, how to fuck, how to make that skin-to-skin connection. I've practiced a lot, and I've learned that the release of oxytocin—along with the feeling of safety it brings—matters deeply for our health and well-being. The emotional and psychological effects on the body, like bonding, intimacy, and relaxation, are powerful and life-giving. That's the stuff I really love. This is what I'm passionate about: being the provider or catalyst for erotic freedom.

What happens during the embrace of sexual connection? I've touched on it throughout this book, but I think there's more to say. Every sexual encounter is layered and unique, like a fingerprint. Our sexual energy is so special, so sacred, that categorizing it can feel like it cheapens the personal meaning it holds for us. Sexual exploration is infinite—it's cerebral, emotional, physical—and there's no shortage of erotic ideas and desires to choose from.

Yet, most of us get into a groove with what we like and stick with it, only veering off the trail now and then for variety. We all have our go-to fantasies and the things that make us go boom. It's one of the greatest gifts of being human: self-pleasure. Very few species have sex for pleasure—dolphins, some types of monkeys—but there's no more visible expression of pleasure than human sexual intercourse.

Many of us feel a craving within, like a hunger, compelling us to seek sexual gratification. We want sex and connection—they aren't separate, even if we pretend they are. Call it hormones, call it eros—it doesn't matter. I'll say it again and again: our sexual pleasure is an important part of our well-being.

The men who come to me want my cock or my ass—or both. They want to be kissed deeply, spanked, touched, pulled close until my breath steams down their necks. But more than anything, they want to feel taken care of, even the ones armed behind their fortress of not-enoughness. They want that deep, raw, creamy load. They want that cock-sized hole filled—not just physically, but emotionally.

If their version of events plays out close to their fantasy, that's a huge win. But it's not as important as you'd think. I'm happy to give it to them, but if I can't connect, even for a moment, if I can't offer trust or a sense of safety, our encounter becomes increasingly difficult to enjoy.

I can't tell you how many times I've been hired to perform a specific set of sexual desires given to me like a menu of options. And 100 percent of the time, the encounter never goes exactly as planned. Once that connection is made, the freedom to explore opens up another adventure altogether.

Is it a phenomenon of the brain, the sexual organs, or hormones? Does it matter? It's what our bodies demand. Whether we're masturbating or having a gang bang at the bathhouse, we will scratch that itch. We always have, and we always will.

The adventure is just beginning for many of us. An intimate relationship with the erotic body is like a healing wound: it keeps regenerating new layers of ecstasy.

As we embrace and honor our desires as sacred, they drive us toward more experiences, more wisdom, more cock, more love, more generosity of service. I've probably said this a thousand times: the secret to the best sexual experience of your life is PRACTICE. Practice, practice, practice!

I'm dubious that anyone ever truly masters sex—not even me. How boring would that be?

BATHHOUSES, SEX PARTIES, HOOKUP APPS—OH, MY!

For generations, we have fought to preserve our sexual freedoms. And while there will always be a segment of the community that turns its nose up at our kinky desires—fearing they tarnish the image of LGBTQIA2+ progress—not everyone wants or needs to fit into a heteronormative mold. After the all-consuming battle for marriage equality, many in the queer community were left out of that conversation. Now, a deeper, more inclusive dialogue is emerging. We are evolving and demanding change in how we connect sexually, emphasizing consent, inclusion, and creating spaces where everyone feels welcome and safe. The good news is that while there is still a lot of work ahead, we are moving forward.

It's 2024. We're fresh out of a global pandemic, and the years of isolation are behind us. The younger generations of queer men are just finding their footing, and while shame and stigma still persist, inspiring changes are taking root. Queer men are demanding the right to explore their sexual freedom now more than ever.

Apps like Sniffies, Scruff, Grindr, Growlr and a wide variety of others—there seems to be an app for every subgroup of queer people—are providing a means to connect and hook up for sex, as well as for sharing information around queer culture. From cum-dump sex parties to good old-fashioned dating, these apps also provide STI testing info and events around the world. Profiles showcase people putting their best faces, assets, and more out there—all in an effort to have their desires met.

Bathhouses, sex clubs, and sex parties are also making a comeback after decades of being shunned, shuttered, and outlawed. The leftover stigma still affects me to this day. Every time I head to a venue, I shake a little from the taboo nature of what it used to be like to enter these spaces. Remember, most of the world saw this as deviant, dangerous, and shameful. Just heading into a sexually charged space can conjure all kinds of anxiety. Have you ever stood in line to get into a bathhouse? The stress is palpable. I try to remember to breathe and be gentle with myself.

Once you're in, you'll discover that while sex is the main event, these spaces have historically been places where we build community and talk quietly in the lounges about current events related to queer culture, arts, and entertainment.

Here are a few things to consider: Consent is sexy. It's much easier to have honest conversations at the sex club now than it was in the days when the hush of the environment took precedence. Asking to touch is no longer done only with an invitational leer. It's often verbalized in casual conversation: "Wow, you're very sexy. May I touch?" Even a silent nod from the person being asked can be a form of consent. The risk of rejection and taking a chance—like touching without knowing for sure if it's OK—may feel a bit lost these days. But in the spirit of safety and service to others, we gladly sacrifice that age-old mental telepathy if it means creating safer, more respectful connections.

Try to use good judgment. Shoving your hand into the middle of two guys having sex at the club is usually frowned upon. Please wait for that invitational look, nod, or glance, then proceed with care and caution. And always be ready to back away.

If you're cruising in the club and you reach out to brush someone walking by as a signal you're interested, wait for them to stop and invite. Groping or blocking their path isn't an invitation at all. Try to find a rhythm—remember, most of us weren't given a handbook on how to cruise. Just feel your way into it. If someone touches you in a way that asks for consent, you get to decide if that feels right for you. Just remember, BE KIND.

Consent can be withdrawn at any time—don't take it personally. Chemistry dictates interaction, no matter how much we think it's about body shape or sexual position. I promise, if the most classically attractive person approaches you, bare naked and ready, but the chemistry's off, the sex won't be fun. Trust me on that. Still, BE KIND.

Not everyone will be your type, and you won't be everyone's type either. Be kind. People will cross your boundaries—not everyone knows how to behave in a sex club. Be kind, but be firm. You may encounter drunk people who needed a little liquid courage to enter. Be kind and stay aware. Smile a lot. There's a jovial energy within you, and while it's easy to fall into anxious interactions, try to access that playful part of you. It will pay off in the end. Maybe this is your chance to practice your inner swagger. I know it can be nerve-wracking, especially if you're new or have been out of the scene for a while. Just remember, BE KIND, especially to yourself

Guess what, you may see a trans person in a sex club or party! Instead of being surprised or questioning who belongs there, say to yourself, "Wow! This is amazing." I can count on one hand how many times I've seen a trans person in a sex club, but that's changing. It's powerful and important that these sacred, beautiful folx feel welcome, especially in inclusive venues for sexual exploration and fun. They belong there just like you do. And remember, you're never required to explore sexually with anyone you don't want to.

As a queer person, you know how hard life can be when you're out on the margins, feeling unacceptable and unseen. Now, it's your turn to be welcoming and loving to our gender-nonconforming family. This topic comes up from time to time, and there will always be those who claim traditions and exclusivity in the name of safe spaces. But I believe we can strike a healthy balance. There are spaces for everyone, and there always will be. So, if you find yourself in a venue where people don't all look like you, BE KIND.

Let's talk about chemsex for a moment. Yes, some people partake in chemsex encounters. Chemsex is defined as using drugs during sex, particularly stimulants like crystal methamphetamine, GHB, MDMA, and many others. Chemsex is viewed as extremely high-risk and frequently portrayed in the media as part of immoral, drug-driven promiscuity. While some of this is true and some sensationalized, it's also true that some queer men use drugs recreationally without succumbing to life-threatening addictions.

Experts say the queer community is experiencing epidemic levels of drug addiction. I don't have the numbers, but considering the marginalization of queer people, it's not surprising. However, with fentanyl now being added to drugs, it's become a whole new level of threat, so I won't argue with the data.

One undeniable fact about drug use and addiction is that stigmatizing individuals has never been helpful. There are significant risks associated with using drugs, especially highly addictive ones. I've watched many lives fall apart from drug addiction that started as occasional party-and-play weekends.

As tempting as it is to dive into harrowing stories of addiction, I'll refer you to my first book, *Every Grain of Sand*, where I share firsthand accounts of my own addiction. It wasn't a party—I lost everything over and over again. I was locked up in jails and institutions, and I never thought my life would spiral so out of control. I was a card-carrying, trash bag over-the-shoulder, screaming-at-trees drug addict. I thought meth was my answer. I was wrong—and, on many occasions, nearly dead wrong.

There's also plenty of information available on chemsex. My friend David Fawcett writes extensively on this topic in his book *Lust, Men, and Meth: A Gay Man's Guide to Sex and Recovery*. If you're struggling with chemsex, it might give you a greater perspective. My message to you, if you choose to partake, is to be mindful, be safe, have fun, and if things go sideways, reach out to people who can help.

Let me be clear: I used meth for twenty-eight years. One thing I've never experienced was casual, social use of meth—it almost always leads to full-blown addiction. If you use it, know that it's not if, but when you become addicted. It's extremely hard to quit, especially with fentanyl in the mix. Use harm reduction sites to get testing kits and supplies, and be careful out there. Always carry Narcan these days. I've been free from active addiction for more than eighteen years, and I carry it in my backpack at all times. It's that serious.

Despite decades of judgment that all sex parties were just drug-addled orgies, there's always been an element of community—we look out for one another. Even in spaces that aren't sober, there's often a communal sense of responsibility among the crowd, with medics on hand in case someone overindulges. The awareness of what works, what is harmful, and how to practice harm reduction is all part of a newer, healthier way to play these days. We're getting really good at teaching each other. No matter the debates about sexually charged events, the information is out there, and consent, inclusion, and safer sex practices are on the marquee.

The good news is, as queer people, we're not hiding in back alleys as much anymore, though some might argue that's a shame. Parks, nude beaches, and cruising areas are packed because we're seeking out ways to commune together more openly. We're taking up space, creating venues, selling out LGBTQIA2+ cruises, street fairs, and hosting sex parties that are not only varied but healthy.

The rise of sober sex parties is a surprising phenomenon. My good friend and mentor, the sexually shameless sex worker Ray Dalton, throws one of the most amazing parties across the U.S. It's called "Fornication" for a reason. He always hires incredible performers who interact with the attendees—they know what they're there for, and we love every moment of it. It's not just about the sex. It's about practice, connection, and meeting men right where they are.

Part of me wants everyone to experience queer sexual freedom, but I also know these spaces and events aren't for everyone. It's easy to fall into the mindset that if you don't enjoy the frenetic energy of a sexually charged public environment, you're somehow missing out or "not gay enough." That's simply not true. You are who you are, and that's beautiful. Exploration is exactly that—a journey to discover what works for you and what doesn't. The invitation is to be mindful of your biases and judgments. Just because something isn't your thing doesn't mean it's wrong for others.

I know plenty of folks who head to Folsom Street Fair, the annual leather kink event in San Francisco, just to hang out and observe. And there are countless guys from around the globe who dive into every aspect of the party scene that weekend. The magic lies in the freedom to explore. What once might've been seen as hedonism is now simply a matter of personal choice. That's sexual freedom!

One thing about your sexual adventure with your body is that it's all yours. You get to decide where, when, and how you wish to explore. There's room to take random loads and have anonymous sex if you want. There's also room for dating—maybe going for a hike is what gets you going, and that's great—make space for it. One is not better than the other. There's room for practice, for awkwardness and stumbling, and there's room for packing up and going home to watch Netflix.

Everyone will have their own experience. There's an endless variety of sexual and intimate relationships out there. If you choose to go on the adventure, you never have to pick just one and stick to it. That is sexual well-being.

SAFER SEX, STDS, AND DOXY-PEP/PREP

One of the things I find fascinating is how much fear of disease prevents us from exploring our sexuality. In the spirit of keeping this book inclusive of the fears and anxieties that create barriers to our sexual freedom and well-being, it would be a huge disservice if I didn't dive into sexual health. Of course, your relationship with your physician and sexual wellness community is always paramount.

It's been nearly forty years since AIDS devastated our community, and we still live with the stigma and fallout of that pandemic every single day. While HIV remains a threat, it no longer keeps us from touching one another. One of our best tools is staying informed. Many men still live in fear, much of it based on misinformation, lack of education, and stigmatizing attitudes.

I can't stress enough how important it is to be well-informed and to take advantage of the science and information available. Access to proactive sexual health is key. There's no shortage of stories of men being shunned and rejected over their HIV status, predicated on misinformation and fear. Still to this day, many people base their well-being on what their friends told them about AIDS transmission—misinformation that could easily be cleared up with a little research.

Let me lay out some basic facts. First, undetectable equals untransmittable (U=U). A simple internet search of U=U will give you hundreds of pages of data on the ten-year-long study showing that antiretroviral drugs (ARVs) suppress HIV to undetectable levels in the blood, resulting in zero transmissions. There were no breakthrough infections from people whose viral load was undetectable. ZERO!

Another tool is pre-exposure prophylaxis (PrEP), which prevents HIV. According to the CDC, PrEP reduces the risk of getting HIV from sex by about 99 percent when taken as prescribed. If you're sexually active, you should be on it. This will be the only time in this book that I "should" you toward something.

Post-exposure prophylaxis (PEP) is taken after a single high-risk event to prevent HIV seroconversion. PEP must be started as soon as possible—always within seventy-two hours of exposure.

DoxyPEP is another preventative treatment, this one for syphilis, chlamydia, and gonorrhea. Think of it as a morning-after pill but for bacterial STIs. Taken as prescribed within 72 hours of condomless sex, Doxy-PEP greatly reduces the risk of contracting these STIs. But it does not help prevent HIV.

While DoxyPEP isn't new, it's just now being adopted as a safer sex protocol. If you're a big slut like me, I encourage you to access it. If you've had fluids exchanged during sex and fear an STI, take DoxyPEP—I suggest before bed that night.

Even if you don't think you need these prevention options, explore them. If you're scared to talk to your doctor, find a local free clinic or do a telemedicine appointment for anonymity. New federal funding grants offer free access to PrEP and other prophylaxis prevention tools. You deserve a stigma-free sex life, and that means staying informed about your sexual health.

This is crucial even if you're selective about your partners. Honestly, the people most at risk are those who don't play much. They might visit a sex club or hook up on Grindr once after a few drinks, but since they don't consider themselves promiscuous, they think they don't need to get tested or take preventive meds. That false sense of security has failed queer men time and time again.

The more promiscuous guys are usually checked more often because they know how to take care of their sexual health. These are the guys you want to know. I love my slutty brothers—they're a great resource when it comes to fun, sexy shenanigans and are often the ones leading the charge in keeping our community informed and safe. Take the recent outbreak of M-pox, formerly known as monkeypox. As a community, we got M-pox under control quickly because we had forty years of experience in dealing with epidemics and wouldn't let media or stigma get ahead of us.

With the internet, social media, and hookup apps, information is easy to find. Relying on secondhand information that shames or stigmatizes others can be harmful not only to you but your community. Even some doctors still shame queer men, insisting that condoms are the only way to prevent HIV when, in fact, they're not all that effective.

So do your homework, stay up-to-date on your bloodwork, and get your STI panels done regularly—even if you haven't had sex recently. It's a good habit to get those labs done every three months. There's nothing shameful about random horny sexual activity, and nothing beats enjoying a hot sexy escapade when you know you're well PrEP-pared.

SEXUAL AWARENESS INQUEERY

For our final exercise, let's explore our experiences in the Room of the Body. As before, there are no right or wrong answers—simply consider these questions and see what comes up. If you like, use a journal to note any thoughts or feelings.

Reflect on the last time you had an orgasm or engaged in sexual pleasure. This could include self-pleasure, a hookup, cruising on the street, a scheduled sex-work appointment (massage, escort, live cam show, etc.), online sexting, sex with a partner, etc.

What stands out about this experience? Were you critical of your body? Were you fantasizing, checking out, being in the moment, engaging in critical self-talk, or considering it an act of self-care? It's OK if you can't remember the details.

Do you have a favorite way to get off, such as watching porn, fantasizing, using toys, getting blow jobs, jacking off, getting penetrated, etc.? Do you feel any judgment about your preferences?

What does it feel like to be in your body right now? What do you appreciate about your body today?

Throughout your day and the week ahead, remember to practice asking empowering questions—and to live in those questions rather than try to answer them. Allow ideas and answers to arrive on their own. Your role is simply to observe and gather insights you can use.

V

IN CLOSING

REMEMBER WHO YOU ARE

Baba Ram Dass traveled all the way to India in search of enlightenment. He became a follower of the Great Maharaji (Neem Karoli Baba). When he arrived, he sat at the feet of his guru and asked, "Maharaji, how can I know God?" Maharaji replied, "Feed people." Ram Dass was so taken aback by this unexpected answer that he thought the translator had made a mistake, so he asked again, "Maharaji, how can I get enlightened?" Maharaji simply said, "Serve people." When I read that story, it hit me like a ton of bricks. Enlightenment isn't some mystical state—it's a state of knowing or understanding.

To know who you are is to remember your essential self, the part of you that can never be changed or harmed. It's not buried deep inside you; it's who you are. Everything else is just an illusion.

I once read that we are all doing only one of two things, even the worst of us. We're either requesting love or expressing love. A big part of me cringes at the New Age phrasing here, but hear me out. Allow me, if you will, to show you who you are with just a couple of simple questions:

When you see someone hungry, what do you wish for them?

When you see someone suffering, what do you wish for them?

I bet it didn't take you long to know the answers. If your first response to someone hungry is to feed them, that's who you are.

You don't need to travel to India or sit on a meditation cushion to understand that. And yes, there are people in the world who are unwell, but I didn't write this book for those experiencing sociopathology or who are incapable of compassion.

What I'm saying is that our humanity isn't lost; it's just been covered up by beliefs and ideas passed down through generations. Even then, it doesn't change our essential self. We will still choose to feed people, every time.

So when the church says we are destined for hell, that we are sinners, or when a parent shows us we are unlovable—we still choose to feed people. When a lover leaves or the breakup happens, we still choose to feed people. When we suffer huge losses and feel hopeless, we still choose, time and again, to feed people.

The unchangeable part of you—that's who you are. And it's the easiest part to connect with.

If we remember who we are, it won't matter if the world says we're too fat, or our cock is too small, or that we're insecure and awkward in the bedroom. There's no program, no path to follow. No matter how ugly you think you are, no matter how much suffering you've endured, no matter what struggles lie ahead—this part of you is unchangeable.

It's the part that can never be taken away. No matter how queer, how sexually frustrated, active or inactive, no matter how your relationships unfold, or how others see you. I beg you to remember who you are.

Who are you beyond your body, beyond your thoughts, beyond all you've been told you are? Who are you beneath the wound? Who are you beyond what is sacred and meaningful to you? You are the person who, when met by someone hungry, will always wish to feed them.

MY WISH FOR YOU

I hope you've found the resources within to imagine your rooms expanding—getting bigger. That the home you're living in feels less cluttered, a bit more clear.

I hope you can take some of this intel with you when you're standing in line at the bathhouse, going on a date with your gym crush, or sitting down for a meal with strangers. And when you're staring into the mirror, taking in all the interesting curves, scars, and beautiful gifts your body carries, I hope you begin to feel like you're sitting at the table among old friends.

I hope you will stay curious about all things sex, love, intimacy, and sexuality. That you will reach out to others and lean into your essential self when things get messy.

I hope you find the wisdom that comes from living a life you've crafted with the remembrance of where you've been and all you've experienced. And I hope you fall madly in love with yourself—not the happily-ever-after kind of love from fairy tales, but the kind where you build a relationship with yourself that can weather being ostracized, where you can come back from stumbling or falling short of your ideals. I hope you'll live beyond the moments when you lied to yourself or made a fool of yourself. Find the parts of you that you've been too afraid to look at and go on a journey together.

I hope you come to see that even the messy, dark parts of you are sacred and important—that the wisdom gained from the hard stuff is what makes your whole house bigger. As you fight inner battles with the parts of you in exile, my hope is that it becomes natural to access the essential part of you that demands compassion. And that you give yourself the same compassion you would offer a suffering stranger. Let none of these battles be in vain.

Finally, I hope you know when to cease fighting and rest. Be deeply appreciative of the miracle that is this life, especially when you least feel like it. Go out and take a few calculated risks. Reach out to someone, and just be present with them. Find your group, your tribe, your little family of gays, and do things together. Know that the sexy swagger exists within you—it exists in all of us. I am with you on this journey, constantly curious, looking inside and all around for what else is possible.

Maybe I'll see you at the sex club or the street fair. I hope you will say hello. Feel free to reach out and touch me—you have my consent.

CRISTIANO ARTE BY LUIGI CRISTIANO
LORO CIUFFENNA, ITALY

VI

THE LAST BREATH

*When I am weak and lying in my final days,
bring me love unlike any other.*

*If I am awake, look deep into my fading eyes and be
certain that I understand that I am loved and desired.*

*When my body fades and my parts are estranged from my
consciousness,*

make love to me like it matters.

*When I am given a few extra moments to be who I am,
waste not one moment of it with small talk. Take my
clothes off, remind me of who I am,*

But don't you dare saint me.

Don't bore me with Hallmark sentiment.

*Speak of the times when we played naked in the clubs.
Danced in the bathhouses. Frolicked in the bushes cruised
in the back alleys.*

Talk about all the things you never say at the dinner table.

Speak of kinky sexy lustful passion.

Remind me that I am a sexual being.

Let me know I am still wanted.

Send in the keepers of the temple.

Bring in the sacred prostitute for he will know who I am.

Prepare me bathe me for my last touch,

Good grief, make sure I remember how to deep kiss, how to touch myself,

Touch me, hold me tightly, and shake my soul loose.

For what a shame it would be to squander the last breath.

Love, David

ACKNOWLEDGEMENTS

There are so many people I want to thank for helping me bring this message to life in this book. This has been a deeply personal journey. At times, I faced bouts of insecurity and paralyzing fear that forced me to practice my own versions of what I wrote about. Yet there were also stretches of excitement and purposeful, intentional days when the words on these pages felt divinely given, as if they were channeled through me. I would read a paragraph and ask out loud, "Who wrote that?" In some ways, I couldn't quite believe what in my bones I knew to be my truth.

People showed up and believed in this project. They invested deeply in reviewing and writing, Zoom calls, transcripts, and deep conversations. They encouraged me, joined me, walked with me—and some even walked away. I also had to make some painful choices, and feelings got hurt. I think that happens when you care deeply about something—all our stuff rises to the surface. All of it matters, and these are the people who made this book possible.

I want to thank my copy editor and writing coach during the initial draft creation of this book, Chris Tebbetts. His early work on this book gave me a cliff to leap from. Like a bungee cord, I was up, down, in, and out more times than I can count. Thank you for helping me find my voice in ways I never expected.

I want to thank Mark, Troy, Jake, J, Dominic, Craig, Brad and Brad, Barry, Josh, Kevin, Paul, Frank, Alex, Diego, Scott and Bamm Bamm, Marqez, Raul, Jeff,

Dean, Wayne, Joshua, Andy, David, Troy, Tim, and Kyle. These incredible men showed up at my home in Palm Springs on Mother's Day weekend for a retreat I spontaneously put together. I wasn't even sure what I was going to do—I just knew I had an idea and needed their help. Many of them also participated in the beta version of the Four Rooms online course. You all represent almost every archetype of the queer person I want to speak to with this book. You taught each other, and me, through unique and fascinating perspectives that influenced many parts of this work.

I'm forever grateful to my mentor, TJ Woodward, for sharing his wisdom with me over the years. He was instrumental in helping me learn to speak this language, allowing me to integrate some of what he shared with me and my own aha moments into the format and exercises in this book. His ongoing encouragement and reflections have been a constant source of inspiration and guidance. Much of how I show up in the world and on these pages is a direct reflection of his work with me and the work he does in the world. Thank you!

To sex workers across the globe who do this work in all its many capacities: I see you. I am one of you. I hope I did our mission justice. I know I gave this my best. Thank you for doing what you do. The world needs you now more than ever.

To all the men I've worked with over the past two decades: without your courage to show up for yourselves and for me, I would not have been able to articulate this message with my whole spirit. You are the reason this book exists now. Your journey is still the dream of someone out there who is still too steeped in shame and fear to seek out the freedom many of you have come to embody. You are the real sages in this book.

I also want to thank those who turned their noses up and criticized sex work as being empty and unhealthy, those who held opinions that sex work was something less than meaningful. Your words and judgments forced me to look deeper and discover how beautiful and sacred this work truly is.

To all the mentors, friends, lovers, and everyday kinsters who model sexual freedom for me every day just by being who you are in the world—thank you.

And Poor Todd, my beautiful partner who cheered me on and never told me my writing sucked (even when it did). Thank you, "Boom Boom," for listening to me read paragraph after paragraph, giving you hours of theory and ruminations about why this word matters or why I can't use that term—especially the baffled look on your face when you didn't even ask about any of that. Thank you for loving my edges and my terrible dad jokes. I love you relentlessly.

To all the bathhouse, sex club, and sex party owners who fight every day to keep their doors open so we have a safe space to practice, explore, connect, and hide out—where we so-called deviants can flourish.

To the content platforms that must navigate government censorship and laws to maintain a safe space for creators to sell their work—your efforts are nothing short of empowering and beautiful.

To the publishers who provide refuge in their catalogs for sexually explicit writers: without you, we would be floundering, hoping to be noticed by those who need to read our work.

To my family and friends who endured years of my struggle, my moments of giving up and starting again, as you watched this book unravel, crumble, and rebuild—I needed to know it would be okay to quit, only to realize I didn't just want to finish this book, I needed to.

Thank you to my own personal Jedi Council. You don't even know who you are, but you are the experts, sages, and icons—the writers, leaders, and facilitators of all things sex, love, intimacy, and sexuality. You kept me honest and curious. You forced me to check my sources, dig deeper, and consider other possible truths. You frustrated me, imprisoned me in my own illusions of inadequacy, and were the cause of deeper inquiry and a new acceptance of my own growth and authority.

Finally, I want to thank my writing coach, mentor, copy editor, friend, and North Star, Heather Ebert. Once again, you showed up when I had no idea what to do next. You held up a mirror for me, called me forward, and helped me own my truth and step into my power. Time and again, you've given me the keys to unlock the writer within. Thank you for seeing this through with me.

Navigating sexual well-being and self-care is a deeply personal journey, and access to reliable resources can make all the difference. The resources listed here aren't exhaustive, but they offer just a few tools, communities, and materials that may support various aspects of your life, from mental and physical health to sexual exploration and safety.

Whether you're seeking support in body positivity, sexual health education, harm reduction, kinky exploration, or simply looking for spaces where you feel seen and understood, these resources offer pathways to deeper exploration.

Remember, the most important resource on this journey is you. This list is merely a starting point—explore what resonates and adapt it as your needs evolve.

CALIFORNIA MEN'S GATHERING

California Men's Gatherings (CMG) hosts seasonal weekend retreats for men to explore personal growth, self-expression, and community in a fun, supportive environment. Often called "summer camp for men," CMG welcomes men of all backgrounds, identities, and orientations, creating a space for connection, belonging, and self-discovery. Open to all men 18+.

https://thecmg.org/

EASTON MOUNTAIN RETREAT CENTER

Easton Mountain is a retreat center and community founded by gay men, offering workshops and events focused on healing, transformation, and the integration of body, mind, and spirit. Set on beautiful, sacred land, Easton fosters a global fellowship that supports personal growth and drives positive change in the world.

https://www.eastonmountain.org/

FLESH & SPIRIT COMMUNITY

Flesh & Spirit is an intentional community of queer men focused on exploring identity, spirituality, and sexuality. Based in San Francisco, the group fosters healing, love, and personal empowerment through workshops and gatherings. Their mission is to transform queer lives by "touching skin, opening hearts, and raising spirit."

https://www.fleshandspirit.org/

GAY MEN'S HEALTH COLLECTIVE

The Gay Men's Health Collective (GMHC) is a volunteer-led organization supporting the health and well-being of gay, bisexual, and men who have sex with men. Focused on sexual health, HIV, HCV, and STI prevention, as well as substance misuse, GMHC promotes healthier LGBT+ communities through active engagement and harm reduction initiatives.

https://gaymenshealthcollective.co.uk/

KINK AWARE PROFESSIONALS (KAP)

The Kink and Polyamory Aware Professionals Directory (KAP), offered by the NCSF, connects individuals with professionals who are knowledgeable and supportive of kink, polyamory, and other diverse sexual expressions. The directory includes psychotherapists, medical experts, legal professionals, and more, all committed to providing nonjudgmental, informed care to the community.

https://www.kapprofessionals.org/

LET'S KICK ASS

Let's Kick ASS (AIDS Survivor Syndrome) empowers long-term HIV survivors by fostering connection, advocacy, and reengagement. The organization combats isolation while addressing the lasting emotional, psychological, and physical challenges faced by survivors. It mobilizes community action to improve quality of life and promote meaningful change.

https://letskickass.hiv/

RADICAL FAERIES

Radical Faeries are a global network of queer and trans individuals united by a shared vision of community, spirituality, and activism. Embracing anti-authoritarian and decentralized principles, they honor the sacredness of nature, celebrate sexual and cultural interconnectedness, and advocate self-expression. Faeries gather in circles and sanctuaries for mutual aid, play, and nurturing, aiming to restore balance within the broader human community.

https://www.nomenus.org/

SAGE ADVOCACY & SERVICE FOR LGBTQ+ ELDERS

For more than forty years, SAGE has championed the rights of LGBTQ+ older adults, ensuring they age with dignity and respect. Born from the activism of the Stonewall era, SAGE continues to provide vital advocacy and services, forming a growing support network for LGBTQ+ elders. SAGE remains a movement of compassionate activists, committed to fighting for the rights of the community's trailblazers who fought for ours.

https://www.sageusa.org/

SAN FRANCISCO AIDS FOUNDATION

San Francisco AIDS Foundation provides essential services, support, and community spaces for individuals of all ages, races, gender identities, and HIV statuses. Prioritizing people living with HIV, LGBTQ+ individuals and those who inject drugs, the foundation also emphasizes care for people of color, those experiencing homelessness, and those with mental health or substance use needs. Their work recognizes the intersections of identity and experience in the fight for health equity.

https://www.sfaf.org/

SF LEATHERMEN'S DISCUSSION GROUP

San Francisco Leathermen's Discussion Group (LDG) is a nonprofit, all-volunteer organization dedicated to the educational needs of the men's BDSM/leather community. Since 1996, LDG has offered guest speakers, workshops, and forums on BDSM techniques, health, safety, relationships, and personal growth. While the group's focus is on leathermen, people of all genders and backgrounds are welcome to attend.

https://www.sfldg.org/

TANTRA 4 GAY MEN

Tantra 4 Gay Men provides workshops, training, and online communities dedicated to guiding men who love men through spiritual, sexual, and personal growth. By offering courses that deepen connections to self and others, Tantra 4 Gay Men encourages intimacy, love, and self-acceptance. Their global and online offerings foster deeper energy, connection, and self-discovery.

https://www.tantra4gaymen.com/

THE BODY ELECTRIC

Body Electric offers transformative, erotic education that integrates sacred and healing practices. Blending Taoism, Tantra, western sexology, psychology, and neurobiology, their workshops use breathwork, touch, and process work to awaken and enhance erotic energy. Participants experience healing, aliveness, and connection to the sacred within a supportive community of learners.

https://bodyelectric.org

THE COMPANY OF MEN

The Company of Men provides essential resources for the gay male massage and sex work community, focusing on safety, health, and support. Originally U.S.-focused, it has since grown into an international community, offering guidance to both providers and clients on best practices, violence prevention, community services, and maintaining overall well-being.

https://www.companyofmen.org/

THE JUNGLE GAYBORHOOD (COSTA RICA)

The Jungle Gayborhood is a queer-centered retreat in Costa Rica designed to foster personal exploration, radical self-expression, and connection—with community, nature, and oneself. Through embodiment practices, sacred plant ceremonies, permaculture, and sacred sexuality, it offers a space for healing and self-discovery amidst lush nature. The inclusive retreat encourages authentic exploration and growth.

https://junglegayborhood.com/

UNBOUND EDITION PRESS

Unbound Edition Press is dedicated to publishing exceptional, often overlooked works, with a focus on elevating marginalized and underappreciated voices, particularly LGBTQ+ and BIPOC authors. Their mission is rooted in a belief in the importance of publishing as a powerful act of advocacy. They are aligned with the efforts of PEN America and belong to the Independent Book Publishers Association.

https://www.unboundedition.com/

WE ARE VILLAGE BERLIN

We Are Village Berlin is a platform for queer individuals to connect, grow, and engage in embodied practices that link queer issues, arts, and societal change. Offering activities for queer masculinities, femininities, and non-binary identities, it fosters inclusivity for transgender, intersex, and gender non-conforming individuals. Programs are accessible globally online.

https://wearevillage.org/

VISIONARY AUTHORS LEADERS AND PROVIDERS

RACE BANNON

Writer, speaker, and community leader in the Leather & Kink world. He is widely recognized for his activism and contributions to the leather community, as well as his advocacy for healthier, more open expressions of sexuality. His work has been influential in bringing greater awareness to kink practices and leather culture.

https://linktr.ee/bannonrace

ALEXANDER CHEVES

Author, essayist, and sex educator. His debut book, *My Love Is a Beast*, became a #1 Amazon bestseller and won the 2022 Geoff Mains Award. He is a contributing editor at *The Advocate* and *Out Magazine*, writing extensively on LGBTQ+ topics, sexuality, and kink.

https://www.alexcheves.com/

RAY DALTON

Sex worker, coach, facilitator, porn star, and personal growth leader. He is an event producer focused on sexual and intimate connection, offering guidance and support to those exploring their sexual identities, relationships, and personal development. Dalton is known for blending erotic work with emotional and spiritual growth.

https://www.shamelessmatters.com

FINN DEERHART

Sex, love, and intimacy coach, writer, and mentor. An AASECT Certified Sexuality Counselor, he offers courses, workshops, retreats, and private sessions where men learn tools to confront limitations, unravel internal shame, and foster deeper connections—grounding themselves into a more profound experience of life.

https://www.finndeerhart.com/

DAVID FAWCETT

Psychotherapist and sex therapist, author of *Lust, Men and Meth* and *Sex Under the Influence*. He specializes in sexual health and addiction recovery, offering insights into the intersection of sex, drug use, and mental health, particularly within the LGBTQ+ community.

https://david-fawcett.com/

JANET HARDY

American writer, sex educator, and founder of Greenery Press. She has published under the names Catherine A. Liszt and Lady Green. Hardy is the author or coauthor of eleven books, often collaborating with Dossie Easton. She identifies as genderqueer, bisexual, and polyamorous.

https://janetwhardyauthor.com/

ARMIN HEINING

Founder of Gay-Tantra® and a pioneer in the field since 1992. He is an international coach and trainer specializing in spiritual and sexual development for men through Tantra practices.

https://www.gay-tantra.eu/

BRENT HEINZE

Licensed Professional Clinical Counselor (LPCC) with more than eighteen years of experience in the mental health field, specializing in working with gay men, couples, and non-traditional relationships. As Executive Director of Perspective Shift, he focuses on producing LGBTQ+ and sex-positive community events. He's also an author and musician.

www.BeginTheShift.org

LANCE NAVARRO

Sacred intimate, massage therapist, and intimacy coach based in St. Pete, Florida

https://www.lancesf.com/

HOLLY RICHMOND, PHD

Somatic Psychotherapist, Licensed Marriage & Family Therapist (LMFT), Certified Sex Therapist (CST), and Certified Sex Therapy Supervisor. She specializes in integrating mind-body techniques to support sexual health, healing, and emotional intimacy. Dr. Richmond's approach focuses on addressing sexual issues through somatic therapy and holistic perspectives to promote deeper, more connected relationships.

https://modernsextherapyinstitutes.com/holly-richmond-ph-d/

KIRK PRINE

Mentor, body story life coach, certified massage therapist, Reiki master, integrative bodyworker, and queer activist. He combines his skills in bodywork, energy healing, and activism to help people reconnect with

their bodies and uncover the stories that shape their lives, promoting holistic healing and self-acceptance.
http://drkirkprine.com/

SAM SEBASTIAN

Mindful somatic therapist working with gay and queer men to address trauma, build secure relationships, release self-limiting beliefs, and foster powerful communication skills. He focuses on helping individuals overcome personal barriers and grow into their most authentic selves, creating opportunities for transformation and meaningful connection in their lives.
https://www.samsebastian.com

WILL TANTRA

Sex educator, performer, and Tantra teacher who focuses on helping individuals maximize both function and pleasure in their bodies. He provides teachings on how to cultivate greater self-awareness, intimacy, and satisfaction through Tantra practices, guiding people toward deeper connections with themselves and others through embodiment and mindfulness techniques.
tantricfitness.com

COURT VOX

Certified Sex & Intimacy Coach, Surrogate Partner Intern, and sacred intimate based in Los Angeles, California. He is the founder of *The Bodyvox*, a platform offering one-to-one coaching, workshops, retreats, and an online community of erotic explorers. His work focuses on helping individuals and couples deepen intimacy and sexual connection.
https://thebodyvox.com

DAVEY WAVEY

Gay guru and storyteller who entertains audiences through humor, open discussions of sexuality, and an unapologetic embrace of gay culture. Using his platform, Davey addresses important issues within the LGBTQ+ community, amplifying underrepresented voices and sharing stories that need to be heard.

www.youtube.com/@DaveyWaveyRaw

TJ WOODWARD

Inspirational speaker, best-selling author, and recovery expert. He is known for his unique blend of spiritual wisdom and practical advice, helping people navigate addiction recovery and personal transformation. Through his work, he empowers individuals to break free from limiting beliefs and embrace a more authentic, fulfilling life.

https://www.tjwoodward.com/

NOTE: This is just a snapshot of the many valuable resources available. The names listed were simply top of mind without any particular hierarchy. Reaching out to any of these people or organizations can help guide you on your journey. Use them as a starting point, then explore further as your needs evolve.

David Wichman is an award-winning author, speaker, and advocate for sexual freedom and expression. Known for his raw honesty and compassionate voice, David's work explores the intersections of shame, desire, and self-acceptance with fearless vulnerability. His memoir, Every Grain of Sand, earned multiple accolades and prestigious awards along with winning the 2024 American Legacy Book Award in LGBTQ+ Nonfiction.

David brings a deeply personal lens to his writing, sharing stories that challenge comfort zones and highlight the complexities of sexuality. Drawing from his 18 years of experience as a male sex worker. His latest book, *The Four Rooms: An InQueery on Sexual Freedom and Well-being*, invites readers to uncover the parts of themselves often silenced by shame and societal conditioning, offering a path and some thought experiments toward deeper connection and self-acceptance.

Through bold storytelling and thought-provoking insights, David opens the door to a conversation about identity, intimacy, feelings of inadequacy and the journey of sexual freedom.

www.ingramcontent.com/pod-product-compliance
Lightning Source LLC
Chambersburg PA
CBHW050820090426
42737CB00022B/3457